The Story of Roth
by Stephen Humphr

London Borough of Southwark
Neighbourhood History No. 6

London Borough of Southwark
Southwark Local Studies Library

ISBN 0 905849 35 3
First published in 1980
New edition 1997
Reprinted with corrections 2004

British Library Cataloguing in Publication Data

Cover Illustrations

Front cover: Entrance to the Surrey Canal from the Thames, 1826
Inside front cover: St. Mary's Church, 1825
Inside back cover: The Free School in St. Marychurch Street, 1826

1. An Introduction to Rotherhithe

Rotherhithe first appeared in history by name in the early 12th century, in the reign of King Henry I. It did not appear in Domesday Book in 1086, when it was presumably considered a part of Bermondsey. From the early Middle Ages, it constituted a separate manor in terms of landownership and a separate ecclesiastical parish (of St. Mary, Rotherhithe) within the Church; and from Tudor times until 1900, the district was also a separate unit of local government as a civil parish run by a body called the Vestry. In 1900 Rotherhithe was once again merged with Bermondsey under the name of the Metropolitan Borough of Bermondsey. In 1965 it became part of the much larger London Borough of Southwark. Rotherhithe had its own Member of Parliament from 1885 to 1950.

Rotherhithe is a district whose history has been closely tied to the sea. Seafaring, shipbuilding, shipbreaking and ship-repairing have all featured prominently in its life. It was the home in the early 17th century of the master of the *Mayflower*, the famous ship of the Pilgrim Fathers, and the place to which the *Temeraire*, a veteran of the Battle of Trafalgar which was immortalised in a painting by J.M.W. Turner, was towed to be broken up in 1838. Nelson's own ship at Trafalgar, the *Victory*, had a Rotherhithe-born chaplain: the Reverend A.J. Scott. Rotherhithe's shipbuilding industry made the district a significant cradle of the Georgian Royal Navy and of the Honourable East India Company's fleet: those two major pillars of England's maritime strength. Ships' masters, ropemakers, mastmakers, anchorsmiths, shipwrights and lightermen all make their appearance in Rotherhithe's records. John Northouck wrote in 1773: 'This village is principally inhabited by masters of ships, seafaring men, with artificers and tradesmen depending upon navigation'. The parish's charity school, which was founded for the sons of mariners in 1613 by two Elder Brothers of Trinity House (another distinguished part of English maritime history), had no fewer than 17 captains among its 37 trustees in 1731. Even Rotherhithe's disasters were maritime in flavour. Whereas the Great Fire of London in 1666 had begun in a baker's shop, Rotherhithe's major fire of 1765 was started when a pitch kettle boiled over. By 1800 shipyards, wharves, and wet and dry docks lined the district's long waterfront, which was connected to the older part of the parish around St. Mary's Church by the long, curving route of

Rotherhithe Street. The enclosed wet docks spread inland rather dramatically in the 19th century, when the Surrey Commercial Docks came to occupy the greater part of the land area of the parish. By 1914 the system had come to comprise nine wet docks, six timber ponds and one end of a canal which stretched for three and a half miles to Camberwell and Peckham. These docks were the home of London's timber trade and of a substantial trade in grain and other foodstuffs. All these aspects of Rotherhithe's maritime history are reflected in St. Mary's Parish Church in St. Marychurch Street, whose site marks the centre of the mediaeval village. Some or all of the mediaeval settlement stood on ground which was relatively high and dry; the rest of the district comprised low-lying land which was liable to floods.

Rotherhithe is very nearly a peninsula, which is bounded on the east side by Limehouse Reach and on the north by the Lower Pool. The land side hinges on Jamaica Road, which leads into Bermondsey, and on Lower Road, which goes to Deptford. Rotherhithe Street follows the peninsula's waterfront for over two miles and was the first district to be developed after the historic heart of the parish. Parts of Rotherhithe Street were once variously called Rotherhithe Wall, Shipwright Street, Trinity Street, Queen Street and Lavender Street. The south-eastern continuation of Rotherhithe Street, Redriff Road, preserves an alternative name to Rotherhithe which was widely used in the 17th and 18th centuries. Samuel Pepys wrote of going 'to Redriffe by water and from thence walked over the fields to Deptford with my wife and her maid agathering of cowslips'. In the following century, Jonathan Swift put Captain Lemuel Gulliver in a house at Redriff: what better place could Swift's concinnity find to fit a sea-captain? Redriff was a pronunciation of an old spelling of Rotherhithe, which had originally meant 'cattle haven'. Rotherhithe Street and Redriff Road provided access to the shipyards and to the pioneering wet dock, known first as the Howland Great Wet Dock and later, when the whaling trade grew, as the Greenland Dock.

The dock survives today as a major inheritance from Rotherhithe's maritime past. That past is well reflected in the names of its public houses and in the fact that so many stood near the waterfront. The late Cornelius Delay listed 155 taverns in the district, of which no fewer than 57 were in Rotherhithe Street. *The Ship* and *Waterman's Arms* were names which appeared several times each. The existing Ship in St. Marychurch Street can be traced back to 1757. Among other nautical names, Redriff Road has the Ship York (dating back to 1809), Derrick Street the Ship and Whale (first recorded in 1767), Rupack Street the Neptune (from 1796), Lower Road the Dreadnought (from 1849) and Canon Beck Road the Lord Nelson (since 1838). The Battle of the Nile stood in Ainsty Street from 1815 to 1931. The Jolly Caulkers (in Lower Road since 1784) recalls a trade from Rotherhithe's shipbuilding days; caulkers made ships' seams watertight. The Surrey Dock Tavern, which was at 163 Rotherhithe Street from 1859 to 1904, had a licensee (John Bell) who made the improbable ascent to the office of Lord Mayor of London (in 1907) and a baronetcy. Another establishment with a slightly different name, the Surrey Commercial Dock Tavern at 1 Redriff Road, was known to sailors for many years as Fitchett's after a licensee early this century. Among the significant taverns on the waterfront itself there were the Torbay, which stood next to Elephant Stairs from at least 1757 to 1955; the Horns Tavern near Cuckold's Point (1731-1896); and the Dog and Duck, in Commercial Dock Passage (1723-1944). The oldest recorded riverfront tavern (and the senior in Rotherhithe generally) – the Angel – is discussed in chapter 3.

No introduction to Rotherhithe can omit a mention of the numerous river stairs. They were the normal means of access to the river for the watermen, who ran the river's small passenger boats of the past. There were up to 20 public ways to the river within Rotherhithe's boundaries, not all of which existed at any one time.

King's Stairs, 1911. The house to the left of the stairs still stands as No. 1 Fulford Street.

The main river stairs were these (going downstream): Rotherhithe or Platform (next to the Angel), King's (near Fulford Street, formerly King Street – see illustration), Prince's, Elephant, Church, Hanover, King and Queen, Globe, Horse Ferry, Pageant's, Horn (at Cuckold's Point), and Dog and Duck. Commercial Dock Pier replaced the earlier Greenland Stairs. From time to time further landing places were named as public stairs, but they do not appear on maps consistently. In the 20th century, especially after the Second World War, Bermondsey Borough Council made moves to have the landing places closed or at least gated; it secured magistrates' approval in cases to which watermen did not object. In an earlier age, such closures would have been seen to reflect a marked anti-commercial policy.

The historic parish of St. Mary, Rotherhithe, consisted of about 754 acres, of which 369 were occupied earlier this century by the Surrey Commercial Docks, and a further 60 by Southwark Park. (The total rises to 886 acres if we measure to the middle of the Thames.) Most of the parish lies between four feet and seven feet below Trinity High Water, and has therefore suffered from flooding over the centuries. St. Mary's Church was rebuilt at least partly because of a flood in 1705. Floods in 1928 and 1953 are well remembered by people who still live in the district.

The parish had a population of 10,296 in the first national census of 1801. In succeeding decades the total rose steadily, most notably after 1841. The total reached 39,255 in 1891, after which it began to slip, although only slightly down to the Second World War. That war led to a drastic reduction. After 1945 the population fell still further because of the decline of local industry, and especially because of the closure of the Surrey Commercial Docks and of the riverside wharves. The nadir was reached in the 1970s. House-building in the past 20 years has seen the population rise again, but it is nowhere near the 19th-century figures.

The western boundary of Rotherhithe was once clearly defined by the mill stream which ran into the Thames at West Lane and which flowed along the eastern side of the present Southwark Park Road. The historic route into Rotherhithe from Bermondsey crossed the mill stream at Mill Pond Bridge. This was not part of the modern Jamaica Road, as one might suppose. The old route turned left into West Lane and Mill Pond Bridge then took it over the stream into Paradise Street. In the 18th century this road was called Old Paradise Street, to distinguish it from New Paradise Street or Paradise Row, which is now the eastern end of Jamaica Road. The fact that the built-up area went no farther south than Paradise Street in the early 18th century shows how small the mediaeval settlement had been. The name 'Paradise' often meant an enclosure and it is just possible that its use at Rotherhithe derives from the enclosure of King Edward III's moated manor house, which was built between Paradise Street and the river in the 14th century and whose remains have been excavated during the last decade.

The mill stream flowed along Southwark Park Road – once called Jamaica Level – towards Galleywall Road. To the east of Southwark Park Road, that is, on the Rotherhithe side, there was a labyrinth of streams, ponds and islands. This district was known as Seven Islands, although there were more than seven islands between the streams. In the early 19th century, one of the islands housed the Swan Tavern, whose situation in old pictures looks extraordinarily rustic, notwithstanding that it was just a few hundred yards from the busy industrial waterfront.

The Swan Tavern, Seven Islands (Southwark Park Road), drawn by J.C. Buckler, 1827.

Galleywall Road was known until 1877 as Manor Road. The manor in question was that of Bermondsey and Deptford Strand, but the road also served as the boundary of Rotherhithe parish. Galley Wall had for centuries before been the name of a causeway or raised road, which ran from south of the Bricklayers' Arms' Goods Yard near Old Kent Road towards Rotherhithe. 'Galley' was sometimes rendered as 'Sallow' or 'Sally', and seems to have come from an old word for a willow. This would make sense as the wall bordered a stream. In the past it was suggested that 'galley' referred to the ships which King Canute is stated to have guided through a channel to by-pass London Bridge, in 1016. It is reasonable to conclude that Canute may have used the natural waterway which flowed alongside old Galley Wall, but for far smaller vessels than 'galley' implies. The waterway was the Earl's Sluice, which joined the Thames south of the Surrey Docks. The Earl's Sluice was the boundary between Rotherhithe and Deptford, and also between Surrey and Kent. Galley Wall extended eastwards (roughly to Greenland Dock) as Long Wall, which was known later as Rogue's Lane and Corbett's Lane (the latter after a murderer whose body was gibbeted there after execution in 1764). The junction between Long Wall and Lower Road was much re-arranged in the mid-19th century.

The land boundaries of Rotherhithe have now been considered. The waterfront will be discussed in the chapters on shipbuilding and on riverside wharves and industries. Two features of the waterfront at the Deptford end, however, merit a mention here, for they do not fall within the scope of the later chapters. One was the 'Condemned Hole' in Odessa Street near Commercial Dock Pier, which was a wharf run by H.M. Customs. In the distant past it was formally known as the King's (or Queen's) Tobacco Ground, and was where contraband tobacco was destroyed. In more modern times it was the wharf of the Receiver of Wreck. This officer dealt with wreck in the broad sense from the whole Port of London: flotsam and jetsam and lagan. Flotsam is floating lost property; jetsam consists of items deliberately thrown overboard (jettisoned) to lighten a ship; and lagan is lost property from underwater. This wharf was once full of such items as hatch covers, barge poles and sweeps, barrels and tarpaulins. Stray items would be collected from the water by a 'drudgerman' or a 'jack-in-the-water'. The wharf was closed in 1962 and a private block of flats called Custom House Reach was built on the site. Some way north of the Condemned Hole, at South Wharf – where the Surrey Docks Farm exists today – the Metropolitan Asylums Board set up an establishment in 1883. It was later taken over by the London County Council. It was intended to be a transfer station for cases of contagious disease such as smallpox. River ambulances took the patients downstream to the isolation hospitals at Dartford (or, originally, to hospital ships). These vessels had tall, thin, black funnels, red crosses on their paddle-boxes, and saloons with windows of frosted glass. George R. Sims wrote of South Wharf in the *Strand Magazine* in 1904: 'Presently we hear a shrill whistle. We look up the street and see an ambulance carriage; the driver has a whistle in his mouth. The signal is answered, the gates of the M.A.B. wharf fly open, the ambulance drives in, and the gates close instantly behind it'. How strange this establishment must have seemed amidst the timber wharves, although on reflection it was just one more use of the river out of the many which form so great a part of Rotherhithe's history.

2. The Parish Church of St. Mary

The present St. Mary's Church was built very largely in 1714-15 by John James. In exactly the same years he rebuilt the church of St. Mary the Virgin at Twickenham. In both cases he retained the tower from the previous church. St. Mary's, Twickenham, still has a 15th-century tower, but here the old tower was replaced in 1747-8 by Lancelot Dowbiggin. Dowbiggin was a rather minor architect whose steeple at St. Mary's, Islington, bears some resemblance to the one at Rotherhithe. John James, however, was a major architect of his day, a successor of Sir Christopher Wren, whose chief London church is that of St. George, Hanover Square.

St. Mary's Church, drawn by Samuel Parsons in 1623: the only known picture of the church before its rebuilding in 1714-15 (reproduced by kind permission of the London Borough of Lambeth Archives Department).

St. Mary's was founded many centuries before 1714. A Rector of Rotherhithe is first recorded in 1282, in the reign of King Edward I, but there was probably a church at Rotherhithe up to a century and a half earlier. Some of the fabric of the mediaeval tower, consisting of clunch (or chalk blocks) and flint, survives under the west end of the present nave; the present 18th-century tower was built to the west of its

9

predecessor. The surviving mediaeval fabric was identified and described in 1913. A picture which is preserved in the Lambeth Archives Department is the sole visual record of St. Mary's before 1714. It shows a building in more than one Gothic style. No doubt the church had been rebuilt and added to at various times since it had been founded.

The church was in decay by the end of the 17th century. Substantial repair was necessary in 1687. What made matters far worse, however, was a flood in 1705. On December 26th of that year the Vestry decided to seek an Act of Parliament to permit the church's rebuilding. Four years later a *brief* was granted to the parish, that is, an authority from the Crown to circulate a letter throughout England to appeal for money to rebuild the church. As a result, Queen Anne's name appears at the head of the list of contributors which the parish drew up (and which is preserved in Southwark Local Studies Library). In 1711, the parish had high hopes of being chosen to benefit from the so-called Fifty Churches Act, by which the government of the day proposed to build or rebuild fifty churches in London. The parish had a novel and compelling argument to present. The money for church-building which Parliament had voted was to come from a tax on coal brought to London. St. Paul's Cathedral had been paid for from the same source. As Rotherhithe's seamen were prominent in carrying that coal, and so in providing the income, would it not be fair to use some of the money to rebuild St. Mary's? Despite this appeal, Rotherhithe failed in its bid and had to be content with the royal brief, numerous voluntary contributions and its regular income from burial dues. Many an 18th-century London parish relied in part on fees paid for burials, in order to rebuild its church.

The appearance of the church has changed much since the 18th century, but the changes have been almost entirely to its interior. Outwardly it is unchanged. Its setting in a narrow street near the river, where it is surrounded by surviving warehouses and by an 18th-century charity school, still strongly reflects the days when Rotherhithe was a distinct part of the Port of London. The charity school whose old building remains opposite the church was founded for the sons of mariners. The building served briefly as the rectory some years ago. The Pacific island prince, Lee

Boo, whose tomb may be found in the churchyard, came to Rotherhithe in 1784 because Henry Wilson, the master of an East Indiaman, lived in a street near St. Mary's, in common with so many ships' captains. Turner's painting, *The Fighting Temeraire*, has a direct connection with the church because the latter now houses furnishings made from the old warship's timbers. The maritime past is finally shown by numerous memorials within the church, above all by that of Christopher Jones, master of the *Mayflower*, the famous ship which took the Pilgrim Fathers to North America in 1620. The memorial dates from 1965.

The church comprises a west steeple, a nave with north and south aisles, a north-east vestry and a shallow projecting sanctuary. It is built of red brick, with stone dressings. The west tower has arched and louvred belfry openings, with clock-faces below and a balustraded parapet above, surmounted by a thin circular stage of Corinthian columns and a short obelisk spire. The steeple was rebuilt in 1861. The projecting east end has a single large arched window. The north and south sides of the church have two tiers of windows. These reflect the north and south galleries which used to exist within the church: the upper tier of arched windows lit the galleries themselves, and the lower tier of segment-headed windows lit the aisles beneath them. Today, only the west or organ gallery survives, for the others were removed in 1876. In the body of the church there are four tall Ionic columns which rise from panelled octagonal bases. The height of the panelling recalls the high box-pews which once filled the body of the church. These, too, were removed in the Victorian period. The architect of these 19th-century changes was William Butterfield. At the east or altar end of the church, there is a Classical reredos or screen of honour for the altar which stands in front of it. The reredos is much the same as it was when new, except that copies of Old Master paintings now adorn the panels which formerly proclaimed the Commandments, the Creed and the Lord's Prayer. Above the reredos, the window has 16th-century German stained glass which depicts the Assumption of the Virgin Mary. The glass was brought here in about 1810.

At the opposite end of the church, in the west gallery, there stands a distinguished organ by John Byfield II, built in 1764-5. Although much restored, it retains its original case and some of its early pipework. The Vestry decided on April 24th, 1764, that an organ 'would be not only a very decent Ornament but also add to the Solemnity of Divine Service'. The first organist, Michael Topping, was elected in December, 1765, and was paid £30 a year. The clock on the front of the organ gallery was made by G. Gulde of Lower Road.

Of the memorials in the church, note particularly the one to the left of the altar to Captain Anthony Wood, who died in 1625. It comprises an inscription below a fine carving of a contemporary ship. On the south wall there is a tablet to Joseph Wade, King's Carver in the naval dockyard at Deptford, who died in 1743. He appears to have been the carver of the reredos in the church. Captain Roger Tweedy, who died in 1655 and who was a principal founder of the parochial charities, was commemorated by an entertainingly appropriate verse on a black marble slab on the north wall: 'His soule A ship with Graces fully laded' and 'Att Rotherheath hee did att length Arrive / and to their poore his tribute fully give / And in this port he doth at anchor stay / hopefully expecting Resurrection's day'. On the opposite or south wall of the church there is a memorial to Henry Meriton of the Honourable East India Company, who died in 1826, after serving as Superintendent of the company's Marine at Bombay for fourteen years. He was involved in a number of skirmishes with French warships in the Napoleonic Wars.

Lee Boo, the 18th-century prince from the Pacific island state of Belau (once known as the Pelew Islands), is commemorated by a tablet within the church and by a tomb outside. He was brought to England in 1784 by Captain Henry Wilson, who lived in Paradise Row, a street which is now incorporated in Jamaica Road. The house in question survived as recently as 1979, when it was demolished by the Greater London Council for a road scheme. Captain Wilson was the master of a ship called the *Antelope*, which belonged to the Honourable East India Company. It was wrecked on Belau on August 9th, 1783, leaving the crew afraid of being attacked by the islanders, for 18th-century seamen in the Pacific sometimes found themselves faced with cannibals. In the event, quite the opposite happened, and the people of Belau proved entirely friendly. It was very fortunate that one of their number was Malayan, who could converse with a Malay-speaking member of Captain Wilson's crew. It was remarkable, too, that the islanders took to the ship's dog, a Newfoundland called Sailor, for they had never before seen a dog, or any four-legged animal save a few rats. When Captain Wilson's men had built a new ship, the king or rupack of Belau (hence Rupack Street at Rotherhithe), called Abba Thulle, asked them to take his younger son, Lee Boo, back to England to learn English ways. For six brief months, Lee Boo was a parishioner of St. Mary's and attended an unidentified academy at Rotherhithe. He died of smallpox on December 27th, 1784, and was buried in St. Mary's churchyard. The Honourable East India Company placed the stone on the tomb (to the left of the south entrance), which reads: 'Stop reader, stop! let Nature claim a tear/A Prince of mine, Lee Boo, lies buried here'. In 1892 a tablet was placed within the church, in the north aisle, by the Secretary of State for India, comparing, in its quotation from the *Acts of the Apostles* (chapter 28, verse 2), the welcome Captain Wilson received on Belau with that of St. Paul when he was shipwrecked on Malta: 'The barbarous people showed us no little kindness'. The Southwark Local Studies Library holds books which were written about the wreck of the Antelope and its sequel within a generation of the events, and they paint an agreeable picture of Lee Boo's character. More recently, Daniel Peacock has published an account, entitled *Lee Boo of Belau/A Prince in London* (South Sea Books, Honolulu, 1987).

Captain Christopher Jones of the *Mayflower* was buried here in 1622. He has a modern memorial in the church. Outside, to the west of the tower, there is a statue by Jamie Sargeant, which was unveiled on July 2nd, 1995, after a service in the church to mark the 375th anniversary of the great voyage. An officer of an American organisation, the National Society, Sons and Daughters of the Pilgrims, unveiled the statue, which represents St. Christopher carrying a child. Back in 1937 a nearby street, Prince's Street, was renamed Mayflower Street.

The many further inscriptions on the walls of St. Mary's record parishioners whose baptisms, marriages and burials appear in the parish registers, which exist from as far back as 1556. They are now kept in the London Metropolitan Archives at Clerkenwell. The church's other possessions include a painting of King Charles I, which reproduces the frontispiece of a book attributed to him, **Eikon Basilike** (the kingly image), and of course the usual church plate, among which may be mentioned a silver salver or almsdish, probably 17th-century, which has fine ornamental detail in several encircling patterns.

Clergy and officials of St. Mary's Church, c.1900. Canon Beck stands in the centre.

The advowson of the church, or right to nominate the Rectors, was bought in 1730 by Clare College at Cambridge. The vendor was the Duke of Chandos. In those days, colleges at Oxford and Cambridge bought advowsons because most of their senior members or **Fellows** were Anglican priests. Consequently, many Rectors of Rotherhithe since the 18th century have been former Fellows of Clare College. The first nominee from the college, Thomas Curling (Rector, 1735-42), was a Fellow from 1723 to 1736. Edward Blick (Rector, 1835-67), who is commemorated by the obelisk near the tower's south door, had been a Fellow from 1812 to 1836. His significant pastoral work at Rotherhithe is recounted in Chapter 10. His successor, Edward Josselyn Beck (Rector,

1867-1907), was a Fellow of Clare from 1855 to 1868 and served as the college's dean from 1860 to 1865. His record of achievement at Rotherhithe was as notable as that of his predecessor, and he left posterity in his debt by writing a history of the parish, entitled ***Memorials to Serve for a History of the Parish of St. Mary, Rotherhithe*** (Cambridge University Press, 1907). It was in Canon Beck's time that Clare College set up a mission in the district; it is discussed in Chapter 10.

3. Landlords and Landmarks

These days we are used to the fact that most properties have separate freehold owners, but even in the recent past a very different order existed, in which large groups of properties belonged to a few individuals and institutions, and were leased out by them. This was true not just of Rotherhithe but of all parts of England. (It is still true of Dulwich within the London Borough of Southwark.) The main estates at Rotherhithe deserve attention, because they had a considerable effect on the life of the district and explain many of the landmarks we can see in Rotherhithe today.

In many parts of this work, the name of Gomm or of Carr-Gomm looms large. For most of the 19th and 20th centuries the lordship of the manor of Rotherhithe has vested in this family. Manorial lordships once implied a jurisdiction, which could be enforced by a court, but this mattered little in Rotherhithe after the 18th century. The manorial estate became an ordinary estate of leased properties. The most celebrated Lord of the Manor of Rotherhithe was Field-Marshal Sir William Maynard Gomm (1784-1875), who owned the estate between 1822 and 1875. He was appointed an ensign in the 9th Regiment in 1794, aged only ten, and went on active service against Napoleon's forces in 1799. He fought under the Duke of Wellington in the Peninsular War; the library has a letter which he wrote to his sister, Sophia, on the eve of the Battle of Vitoria (in Spain) in 1813. After the Battle of Waterloo (in which he fought with Picton's division), he was made a Knight of the Bath and a lieutenant-colonel in the Coldstream Guards. He served in England for over 20 years and was then sent successively to Jamaica, Mauritius and India as Commander-in-Chief. He ended his days as Constable of the Tower of London and as Colonel of the Coldstream Guards. Gomm Road and the former Maynard Road were named after him, and there were once two public houses called the Sir William Gomm (in Abbeyfield Road and the former Commercial Street).

The estate which Sir William inherited in 1822 may be divided into two parts. There was what we might call an urban part, which consisted of the south side of Paradise Street, the eastern end of Jamaica Road (then called Paradise Row), the part of Cathay Street which connects the two, plus an ancient but now vanished road called Clark's Orchard. All this was more or less built over. To the south, however, there was the rural part of the estate, including most of the land between Jamaica Road, Southwark Park Road, Galleywall Road, Long Wall (roughly Rotherhithe New Road) and Lower Road, plus several large fields on the eastern side of Lower Road as far as the King's Mill Stream. When Sir William inherited all this land, there were only half a dozen buildings along Lower Road, and just two or three elsewhere. The whole area was otherwise pasture or market garden ground.

The Jolly Sailor Public House, Lower Road, c.1891.

Sir William's open land was divided into named fields. Paradise Field lay south of Jamaica Road, and Windmill Field and Musick House Field were farther south. These three fields, totalling 37 acres, were leased in 1780 to Thomas Brandon, a market gardener, whose family owned substantial lands in Walworth. In Lower Road, on the park side, lay Cock and Pie Field. This was named after a public house which stood in the 18th century on the other side of the road, in a smaller plot of land called the Shoulder of Mutton Field. In those days it was an isolated spot on the road to Deptford. In 1776 the public house was leased to Jonathan Oldfield, described as 'tea dealer and chinaman', and he was evidently responsible for changing the tavern's name to the China Hall, which it retains to this day. In the field next to it in 1776 there was 'a wooden building used as a concert room or playhouse', which attracted the Vestry's stern disapproval.

There, its members complained, 'are frequently represented Plays and Interludes to the disturbance of the Neighbourhood and the Vitiating the Morals of their Workmen and servants'. The theatre lasted only a couple of years. Another old public house stood on Sir William's land in Lower Road: the Jolly Sailor. It stood from at least 1780 until 1945 in front of Brandram's works (see chapter 6) and the library has a 19th-century photograph of what was evidently the original building. At a much later date, a well-known place of entertainment stood opposite: Terriss's Theatre, which was opened in Lower Road in October, 1899, between St. Olave's Hospital and St. Mary's School. It was named after the murdered actor, William Terriss. The younger George Conquest leased it in 1900 and supplied the theatrical fare common to establishments in south London: melodrama, pantomine and popular plays. In 1907 it changed to variety and was renamed the Rotherhithe Hippodrome. From 1930 it was a cinema and lasted in that role until the Blitz. The building was demolished in 1955.

During Sir William's ownership, the estate which has been described was rapidly developed, with the exception of Southwark Park. The main roads were developed first, and afterwards, in the third quarter of the century, many new side roads were formed, especially south of Southwark Park, around Abbeyfield Road. The day-to-day running of the estate was in the hands of a steward; after 1822 this office was always filled by a member of the Still family, solicitors of Lincoln's Inn.

Field-Marshal Gomm left the estate to his wife, and she in turn bequeathed it to her niece, Emily Blanche Carr, in 1877. The new owner took the additional name of Gomm. She was the wife of Francis Culling Carr (hence Culling Road) and lived near Maidenhead in a house called Redriff. Her son, Hubert William Carr-Gomm, was the Liberal Member of Parliament for Rotherhithe from 1906 to 1918, and served as private secretary to Herbert Asquith, the Prime Minister. The family held the estate until the 1960s, when all such estates of poorer, residential property became economically dubious (and subject to numerous compulsory purchase orders by councils). A recent member of the family, Richard Carr-Gomm, who was not the owner of the estate himself, lived in Rotherhithe for a time and founded in succession two housing associations: the Abbeyfield Society (after a road on the estate) and the Carr-Gomm Society.

The Dukes of Bedford owned a significant estate of 139 acres on the eastern side of Rotherhithe. Its acquisition in 1695 by the first Duke's heir through his marriage to Elizabeth Howland is discussed in chapter 4. In the early 18th century the estate consisted of the Howland Great Wet Dock – the forerunner of the present Greenland Dock – and properties at the lower end of Rotherhithe Street, south of Nelson Dock, with some fields to their west. A map of the estate in 1743 exists. The dock was sold in 1763, but other parts of the estate were kept until the early 1800s. At one time Derrick Street was called Russell Street after the family name of the Dukes of Bedford. Land in the vicinity of Lower Road, Bush Road and Rotherhithe New Road has for centuries been part of the Ram Estate, whose owners were Lords of the Manor of Bermondsey and Deptford Strand until the late 1980s. The original core of the estate was a large part of the site of Bermondsey Abbey, adjoining the present Tower Bridge Road. The two large fields at Rotherhithe, called Yeoman's Croft and the Hawthorn Bush, must have once been outlying properties of little consequence. Later, however, they were built over and became much more valuable. The mention of Bermondsey Abbey makes it opportune to point out that the monastery once owned most of Rotherhithe. About one half of the parish was given to it by King Henry I (reigned 1100-35) in the early 12th century. The other half went to the king's illegitimate son, Robert, the Earl of Gloucester, after whom the Earl's Sluice was probably named. Eventually the abbey acquired his half, too. The monastic estate came to an end in 1538, when King Henry VIII dissolved Bermondsey Abbey as part of his abolition of monasteries throughout England.

In the heart of the mediaeval village, it is clear that there were many smaller properties which were independent of the abbey. King Edward III's manor house was the most important of them. This was a substantial residence which was built between 1353 and 1361 (chiefly in 1353-6) on a site bounded by Cathay Street, Rotherhithe Street, the present Millpond Estate and Paradise Street. It consisted of a wharf on the riverfront, a principal or northern courtyard which was built of stone, a subsidiary or southern courtyard which was surrounded by earthen walls, and a large garden. Parts of the footings of the northern and eastern ranges of the principal courtyard may be seen exposed today, following excavations in the 1980s. Beyond them lay a moat, which does not seem to have been filled in until the later 1600s. The garden, which contained vines in King Edward III's time, may well have led to the local use of the name 'paradise', which was once a normal word for enclosed garden ground. The king's own chamber was undoubtedly in the northern courtyard; it is interesting to note that in 1353 a partition was put into it 'for the king's falcons to perch on'. The chamber of 'the lord prince', that is, Edward, the Black Prince, the victor of Poitiers, was also apparently placed in this courtyard.

King Edward III's property passed into monastic hands after his death but returned to the Crown in the 16th century. It was then leased out in a complicated series of transactions, from which three facts may be extracted. One is that in the late 16th and early 17th centuries, the former royal mansion was in the hands of Peter Hills, mariner, who founded the local charity school (see chapter 10). An acre of meadow called the barn close was part of the property and had lately been occupied by one John Clark, who probably gave his name to Clark's Orchard. Secondly, for much of the 17th century, a part of the old mansion was used to manufacture delftware, the blue and white tin-glazed earthenware which was once made in many pothouses along the Thames. Finally, in the late 17th century, when the Jesson family owned the property, the latter included 'a messuage commonly known by the name of the sign of the Angel situated near Redriffe Stairs'. This is none other than the doyen of Rotherhithe's taverns, which is now situated on the waterfront. In 1682 it was placed diagonally opposite its present site, and stood between the filled-in moat of the old mansion and what is now Cathay Street. The filled-in moat had became an alley by which the tavern could be reached. It is tantalising that a token coin issued at Rotherhithe in 1668 came from 'the Salutation'; this is an old name for the Annunciation, in which the Archangel Gabriel announced the Incarnation to the Virgin Mary. Could the Salutation be the Angel, and thus make it possible that the sign went back before the Reformation? If so, an already venerable public house would be put into a more distinguished antiquity.

The Angel Public House, with Rotherhithe or Platform Stairs to the right of it and the Platform Engineering Works of Wilmott and Cobon in the background.

Near the Angel there is a short stretch of street called Mayflower Street, which had been called Prince's Street from its formation in the early 18th century until 1937. This street formed a small but important estate, whose origin and ownership need to be researched further. Until the Second World War it remained an intact street of unusually grand Georgian terraced houses. For long after their erection, they were occupied largely by ships' masters. In the early 1840s, for example, Captain James May, Captain George Lulham, Captain William Phillips and Captain Thomas Skey are all stated in St. Mary's registers as living in the street. Some of the houses were destroyed by bombing and the rest were gradually demolished after 1945. If the street had survived, it would undoubtedly have been regarded in recent years as Rotherhithe's architectural showpiece.

If Prince's Street was the showpiece of urban Rotherhithe, St. Helena Gardens occupied the role of chief rural attraction. The gardens existed between 1770 and 1881, in the vicinity of the present St. Katherine's Church, Eugenia Road. This was an isolated spot for much of that period, and the gardens therefore offered an attractive retreat from the crowded and noisy city. They offered the standard fare of London's Georgian and Victorian pleasure grounds: music and dancing, refreshments, agreeable gardens and fireworks. In this case, exceptional views could also be claimed for the establishment. The gardens came to an end as Rotherhithe became a fully-built-up part of London, and this interesting small estate disappeared beneath streets of terraced houses.

Prince's Street, 1934.

4. The Surrey Docks

The first wet dock in London was opened at Blackwall in King Charles II's reign and was later called Brunswick Dock. Rotherhithe had the distinction of being the site of the second and more important wet dock. It was built under an Act of Parliament of 1696 on behalf of the Duke of Bedford's family, the Russells. The Duke's heir (the Marquess of Tavistock) had married Elizabeth Howland, daughter of John Howland of Streatham, on May 23rd, 1695. John Howland settled on his son-in-law an estate at Rotherhithe, consisting of several dozen acres fronting Limehouse Reach from the border with Deptford to where Nelson Dock House now stands. The new dock, which was known as the Howland Great Wet Dock, was finished within four years.

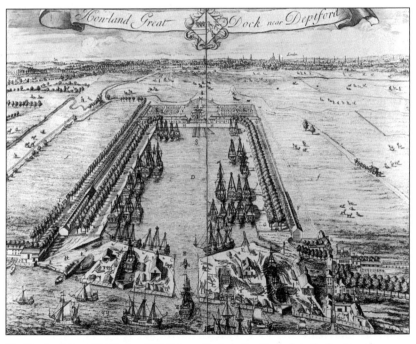

The Howland Great Wet Dock, c.1700 Note particularly the shipyards in the foreground.

A print of about 1700 shows a bird's-eye view of the dock. It is tree-lined to protect ships from storm winds, and has a substantial house or mansion at its head, but there are no warehouses or high enclosing walls such as 19th century docks were given. Its surroundings are almost entirely rural. What it offered was a safe haven from storms, plus facilities for masting and dismasting, and for careening ships (cleaning and repairing their hulls and keels). After the notorious storm of 1703, which damaged many ships in the Thames, it could be claimed with pride that just one ship had been *slightly* damaged in a dock which could hold '120 sail of the largest merchant ships'. The dock was managed for the Dukes of Bedford by the Wells family, two of whose members, John (1662-1702) and Richard (born 1664), lent money for its construction. The Wellses were prosperous shipbuilders at Rotherhithe for more than a century. They built many 74-gun ships of the line for the Royal Navy, which were the largest warships to be built in private yards. In 1763 John and William Wells bought the Howland Great Wet Dock from the fourth Duke of Bedford for £18,000. The space was turned over for the use of Greenlandmen engaged in the taking of the black whale, and the dock was renamed the Greenland Dock. Blubber was boiled there for oil. By the early 19th century this trade had declined, whereas the timber trade had burgeoned.

The next changes of ownership of the dock reflected these circumstances. The Southwark Local Studies Library possesses copies of the deeds by which William Ritchie bought the dock in 1806. The vendors were John Wells (1761-1848) and William Wells (1768-1847) – who were at that time partners in the shipbuilding firm of Perry, Wells and Green at Blackwall and their brother, Admiral Thomas Wells. William Ritchie was a timber merchant from Greenwich. In the year after his acquisition, the Commercial Dock Co. was formed, to buy the property in turn and to compete in the timber trade. Between 1811 and 1815 the company opened four more, smaller docks to the north of the Greenland Dock, which were later known as Norway and Lady Docks, and Acorn and Lavender Ponds. Timber was floated in the ponds to remove the sap and as a method of storage. The new firm also built many granaries, for from the beginning the trade in grain was almost as significant as that in timber. A book on the Commercial Docks written in 1844 by a director of the company, Nathaniel Gould, remarks in particular that two big granaries had been built of Canadian pine timber. Canada and the Baltic states were the places of origin of the docks' timber.

Before the Commercial Dock Co. took over the Greenland Dock, another enterprise had been launched just to the west. Rotherhithe witnessed a late example of canal mania in the form of Ralph Dodd's Grand Surrey Canal. Dodd was a visionary engineer who dreamt of connecting Rotherhithe with Portsmouth by a canal. His scheme won parliamentary approval in 1801 and work began in 1802. Dodd soon lost his power over the scheme, but that of Sir John Hall, a prominent shipowner, grew. It was under his influence that the Rotherhithe end of the canal was provided in 1804-7 with two elongated or acicular docks, which he considered to afford commercial benefit. Hall's own brig, the *Argo*, was the first vessel to enter the new development, dressed overall and embarking a military band which played *Rule, Britannia!*

The canal was completed to Camberwell Road in 1811 and a branch to Peckham was added in 1825-6, but the cut to the Thames at Vauxhall was never undertaken and the ambitious route towards the south was not pursued. Market gardening was the canal's main initial source of income, rather than timber, but such was the prospect of profit from the timber trade at Rotherhithe in the early 1800s that two further enterprises attracted capital in order to rival the Commercial Dock Co. One, which built the East Country Dock south of the Greenland Dock in 1807, remained a separate concern until 1850, when its business was bought for £40,000 by the Commercial Dock Co. The other, the Baltic Dock Co., was formed in 1809, but was bought out by the Commercial Dock Co. before it could become an active rival. It was a particular threat because its promoters had secured a promise from the Treasury of a preference in bonding timber.

These dock companies initially made good profits – the Commercial Dock Co. paid 8% in 1814 – but then slipped back. For many years 2% or 3% was a normal return. Profitability improved in the mid-century. The Commercial Dock Co. paid 4% from 1847, 5% from 1852 and reached 6% in 1863. The Grand Surrey Docks and Canal Co.'s dividend rose from 2% to 6% between 1847 and 1862. It came to be feared that this success could not be sustained, and so negotiations began to amalgamate the businesses. This was effected on January 2nd, 1865, under the name of the Surrey Commercial Dock Co. Capital investment was substantial in the following years. In 1866 a connection was made between the two old systems. Then James A. McConnochie superintended the building of the substantial Canada Dock, which opened in 1876 and was provided with granaries capable of holding 35,000 tons. The Port of London Authority's archive, which is now held by the Museum in Docklands, includes some very interesting photographs of the building of this dock. Its opening brought the system to a total of nine docks and six timber ponds, comprising 176 acres of water and 193 acres of wharfage, making 369 acres in all. The dominance of this enterprise in Rotherhithe's economy is obvious enough. As early as 1843, the Commercial Dock Co. alone could claim to pay about one fifth of the parish's rates.

A generation after Canada Dock had opened, there came the considerable extension of the Greenland Dock. It was lengthened towards the west to be 2,250 ft. long, crossing the line of the old Surrey Canal and connecting with the Canada Dock. It was also given a massive new lock, 550 ft. long, which was capable of receiving the largest steamers. All this was carried out between 1895 and 1904 under Sir John Wolfe-Barry, the engineer who built Tower Bridge, at a cost of nearly £1 million. This huge scheme allowed for the handling of general cargo as well as timber. A few years later, in 1909, the Port of London Authority was set up to take over all the independent dock companies, and that authority ran the Surrey Commercial Docks down to their closure in 1970.

Some 80% of the Port of London's timber trade passed through the Surrey Commercial Docks. In 1904 enough wood was received there to gird the entire Equator with it to a width of three and a half feet. Timber was normally measured by the *standard*, which consisted of 1,980 board feet, each of which was 12 ins. by 12 ins. by 1 in. One standard weighs about two and a half tons. The ships which brought the timber were not very large for most of the 19th century: up to 500 tons on average down to 1875. These ships were minute in contrast to the big steamers for which the Greenland Dock was prepared at the end of the century, and which became regular visitors in the 20th century. Cunard White Star A Class liners of 14,000 tons made their way to Rotherhithe between the

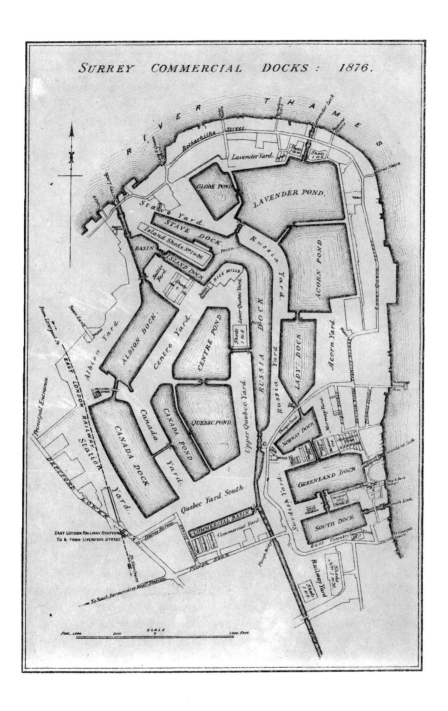

SURREY COMMERCIAL DOCKS : 1876.

27

The Surrey Commercial Docks, 1926. Nelson Dock may be seen in the foreground.

wars and were among the largest vessels to reach so far up the river. The Canadian Pacific Line, the Allan Line and the Thomson Line also used the Surrey Commercial Docks regularly earlier this century, to embark passengers as well as to bring cargoes. They sailed between Rotherhithe and Canada, where they called at ports on the St. Lawrence River, Halifax in Nova Scotia and St. John in New Brunswick. In contrast to the huge transatlantic vessels, there were wooden sailing ships even in the 1930s which plied from the Baltic and which were known as 'onkers' from the particular sound of their deck-mounted windmill pumps. They were barques and barquentines of 800 to 1,200 tons, and brought their cargoes of timber to Rotherhithe in the summer months. We must remember too that barges or lighters were also very numerous. The so-called 'free-water clause' in the Acts which set up London's dock systems, by which lightermen could enter the enclosed docks without charge, led to the ubiquity of barges in the Port of London. In 1840, when 735 sea-going vessels entered the Commercial Docks, no fewer than 7,799 barges and small craft accompanied them. The picture was the same in the 20th century. Modern views of the Greenland Dock always show large cargo ships in the company of barges, sometimes all but surrounded by a dozen and more of them.

The characteristic dock workers in timber were the deal porters. Theirs was a skilled trade, and one which required considerable fitness and stamina. The height of the timber which they had to stack could reach 50 ft., and as a result of carrying long planks at that height, they were given the nickname of 'Blondins', after the great tightrope walker. Deal porters wore distinctive leather hats with long flaps, which were intended to protect the shoulders. After the Second World War their work was mechanised.

Reference was made above to the importance of the trade in grain. At times there were in fact far more ships carrying grain than those carrying timber. In 1840, for example, of the 735 sea-going ships which entered the Commercial Docks, no fewer than 476 were grain-carrying vessels but only 211 were timber-importing ships. The latter, however, steadily increased in size during the 19th century, whereas grain vessels remained relatively small. Ships of about 150 tons were normal in the grain trade for many decades after the docks had opened. In 1876, the Surrey Commercial Docks saw 1,213 ships of the timber trade, carrying 599,518 tons between them, against 426 grain vessels holding 142,835 tons.

In common with the dock systems on the north bank of the Thames, the Surrey Commercial Docks suffered greatly in the Second World War. The great timber sheds were destroyed, and warehouses were burnt out. After 1945, a remarkable recovery took place throughout the Port of London, and the late 1950s saw a new height of prosperity. Subsequent decline came swiftly. A combination of new methods of cargo-handling and a considerable increase in the size of ships led to the migration of the port downriver and the closure of all the upriver dock systems. Palletisation, or the use of pallets to hold large loads for lifting by machine, was an early major change after the war. In 1958 there came 'timber packaging', or the handling of timber in packaged quantities. Bulk carriers were then introduced which dwarfed earlier ships in the trade. They could reach 30,000 tons. Such ships could not enter the Surrey Commercial Docks.

In 1966 No. 34 Berth at Tilbury was opened to receive these new timber ships, after considerable building work. It had a capacity of 5,000 standards of timber. Within a year, two more berths at Tilbury (Nos. 42 and 44) were laid out to handle the arrival of packaged timber in bulk carriers. One ship, the Atlantic City, delivered 24,000 tons of cargo at No. 42 Berth in one visit in 1967, including no fewer than 4,600 standards of softwood. All these momentous innovations, which were the timber trade's equivalent of containerisation, led to the closure of the Surrey Commercial Docks in 1970, and as a result a massive area became vacant for the first time since the early 1800s.

5. Shipbuilding and Shipbreaking

A few years ago a letter was received at Southwark Local Studies Library from a researcher who was studying the career of an 18th-century officer in the Royal Navy. The officer had served as a midshipman or lieutenant in three ships, *Chesterfield, Sphynx* and *Tartar*, and it had emerged that all three had been built in shipyards at Rotherhithe. Few enquiries could so neatly emphasise the importance of shipbuilding in the district, or the major contribution which Rotherhithe made to the Royal Navy in past centuries.

The *Chesterfield* was a 44-gun, 4th-rate warship, which was launched in October, 1743, from the yard of John Quallet at Pitchers Point, roughly opposite the Amos Estate in Rotherhithe Street. The *Sphynx* was a sloop of 24 guns, which was launched from Allen's yard in December, 1747. The third ship, the *Tartar*, was also a sloop, but with 28 guns, and was launched at Randall's yard in April, 1756. Randall's was a much more important firm than the other two. Under the names of Randall, Randall and Brent, and Samuel and Daniel Brent, it occupied three separate yards: one is best known as Nelson Dock and is the only Rotherhithe shipyard to survive physically to any extent; and the remaining two flanked the entrance to Greenland Dock. All three yards appear on Horwood's map of 1799 as Randall and Brent. The firm built a considerable number of vessels for the Royal Navy and for the Honourable East India Company between the mid-18th century and the 1820s, including up to a dozen 74-gun warships. These were 3rd-rate ships of the line and were the largest ships to be built for the Royal Navy in private yards.

It is comparatively easy to establish lists of ships built at Rotherhithe for the Royal Navy and for the Honourable East India Company, for their records are national records and are extant and accessible. Records of merchant shipbuilding, however, are relatively few and elusive. They tend to be late in date, too, making it difficult to investigate the 18th century and all but impossible to research the 16th and 17th centuries. The present state of research therefore distorts the history of shipbuilding at Rotherhithe (and elsewhere on the Thames) towards warships and East Indiamen, and in favour of the 18th and 19th centuries at the expense of a considered verdict on all periods. What can definitely be said to emerge is the fact that Rotherhithe's shipyards flourished notably as a result of the various wars which were fought between the 1690s and the time of Waterloo. These wars were fought chiefly against the French, beginning in the time of Louis XIV and ending with Napoleon. Given that the Seven Years' War (1756-63), for example, was fought in Canada and in India, and that the French Revolutionary and Napoleonic Wars (1793-1815) were worldwide, there was a huge increase in demand for naval vessels, which could not be satisfied in the Royal Navy's own dockyards. Randall and Brent's list of warships is considerable in the 1790s and early 1800s. Conversely, all the yards lost most of this business after 1815.

The one fact which stands out from the early history of shipbuilding at Rotherhithe is that in 1612 a charter was granted to 'the Master, Wardens and Comynaltie (Community) of the arte or misterie of Shipwrightes of Redrith in the Countie of Surrey'. This was in opposition to the older body of Free Shipwrights, who seem to have been centred at Ratcliff across the river. It is extraordinary that a new guild should have won formal royal approval in rivalry with an existing City guild. The charter testifies to the value of shipbuilding at Rotherhithe and to its establishment well before 1612. There is a reference in government records 20 years later to the shipwrights of Rotherhithe having the power to survey shipbuilding outside the parish, which reinforces the impression of an influential and prosperous trade. Stray mentions suggest that it went back at least to the early 16th century, roughly to the time when naval shipbuilding is known to have begun downstream at Deptford and Woolwich.

It must be remembered that ships were very small down to the 18th century, and even in the 19th century many classes of vessel were easily accommodated in yards on the Thames. In the previous chapter it was noted that grain ships averaged no more than 150 tons in the first half of the 19th century. Large numbers of cargo ships and smaller warships amounted to no more than a few hundred tons. If such vessels could be built at Rotherhithe, they could clearly be repaired there and eventually be broken up there. Builders, repairers and breakers made up the greater part of the riverside economy for a couple of centuries, sometimes succeeding one another on an individual site.

There were about a dozen major yards at Rotherhithe, of which some details are known from the 18th and 19th centuries. The majority of them occupied a relatively small stretch of the riverfront, from just downstream of Surrey Lock to Pageant Stairs. Immediately downstream of Surrey Lock there were the premises of John Beatson, Rotherhithe's best-known shipbreaker. He succeeded to a business which had been run by his father, David, and ran it until his death in 1858. His fame arises chiefly from J.M.W. Turner's painting, *The Fighting Temeraire*, which showed the ship being towed to Beatson's yard to be broken up in 1838. The painting itself is not an accurate depiction of the ship (or even of the tug!), and it undoubtedly romanticised the vessel. It is sometimes claimed that in the absence of Turner's painting, the *Temeraire* would be forgotten. Such an argument would be extreme, for the vessel played a significant part in the Battle of Trafalgar. Captain Sir Eliab Harvey, who commanded her, was one of only three individuals named in the House of Commons' vote of thanks in January, 1806 (the others being Nelson and Collingwood). Southwark Local Studies Library holds the journal and ledger from Beatson's yard, in which the transaction to break up the *Temeraire* is recorded. She was a Chatham-built, 98-gun ship of the line. The ship's timbers went partly to make two chairs, a table and altar rails for St. Paul's Church off Rotherhithe Street, which was a chapel of ease to St. Mary's from 1850. William Beatson, the shipbreaker's brother, is said to have built it. The furnishings were moved to St. Mary's after the Second World War. Another famous warship from Nelson's time, the *Bellerophon*, was also broken up at Rotherhithe, in 1836. She was the vessel on which Napoleon had begun his journey into exile on St. Helena in 1815. A shipbreaker's yard typically consisted of a wharf on the riverfront, with a larger piece of ground on the other side of Rotherhithe Street for the storage of timber. John Beatson's yard included a small dock. A deed of 1811 in the library has a plan of the property of a shipbreaker called Job Cockshott. He leased Quebec Wharf, plus land opposite between Lavender Lane and Lavender Place (near what is Lavender Road today). Various buildings on that side of Rotherhithe Street were included in the lease, among them the Swallow Galley public house on the corner of Lavender Place.

By the site of Beatson's yard, Rotherhithe Street turns inland, and it did so to go round Bull Head Dock. This is the property which is marked as 'Mr Woolcombe's Yard' on Horwood's map of 1799. The library holds various Victorian deeds of the dock. In one, of 1839, it was leased by John Hague, an engineer, for a rent of £216 a year. In another from 20 years later, John Brown and Robert Barclay Brown, shipwrights, leased it for £275 a year, with a promise to spend £2,295 in enlarging and improving it. The value of such deeds centres particularly on the plans which they include. By the end of the 19th century, Bull Head Dock had become the Vestry's dust wharf. The next yard downstream was labelled 'Mr. Mestaer's Yard' in 1799. He was Peter Mistaer (the name is variously spelt), who built the narrow and curving alleyway opposite, called Mistear's Buildings. The *Daily Advertiser* of May 14th, 1804, reports the launching from Mistaer's yard of 'a very fine East Indiaman' of 600 tons; it adds, 'immediately after she was launched she was brought into the Basin, on the opposite side of the Yard, to be coppered'. The coppering guarded against fouling.

Mistaer's yard is shown in a painting in the Tate Gallery. Sometimes his yard was called Princes Dock, but in 1843 it was called the King and Queen Ship

Mistaer's Buildings, Rotherhithe Street, c.1935.

34

Yard (for the King and Queen public house and King and Queen Stairs were just upstream). It was then in the occupation of George Hawks. He was either the son or brother of Edward Hawks (died 1844), whose memorial may be seen in St. Mary's Church: 'This Tablet / Was erected by the workmen / And late apprentices of / Mr Edward Hawks / For many years an extensive / Ship builder in this Parish / As a Testimonial / Of grateful remembrance / For his kindness and urbanity / of manners'. Edward was the younger brother of Sir Robert Shafto Hawks, a partner in the Gateshead Ironworks near Newcastle-upon-Tyne. Edward's son, Robert Shafto Hawks, became Vestry Clerk of Rotherhithe later in the century. For a few years he shared this office with his brother-in-law, James J. Stokes. The brother-in-law in turn was married to Agnes Beatson, daughter of the shipbreaker. A tightly-knit community!

The next yard downstream, confusingly, was also called King and Queen Dock. Beyond that there came Upper Globe Dock (or Sweeting's Dock). A sale catalogue of about 1850 in the library mentions that this dock had a river frontage of 280 ft. and states that it then comprised 'a building slip and large dry dock, spacious engineer's factory, pitching house, saw pit and loft over, three messuages, oakum store and, next the street, a brick-built dwelling house, containing 12 rooms and a counting house'. This was all upstream of Globe Stairs; *Lower* Globe Dock lay downstream. The latter property was in the hands of John Small Sedger in 1843. He lived nearly opposite, in Beatson Walk (previously Globe Lane), and had been a ship owner before running dry docks at Rotherhithe. He became a considerable landowner in the district.

The next two docks were near Horse Ferry Stairs. Horse Ferry Dock was immediately upstream and belonged to John Thompson, 'boat builder', in 1843. This site was one which was extensively developed at a later date, for the group of workshops of 1843 had been replaced by a substantial dry dock by 1868. These premises remained in use until the 1930s. Downstream of Globe Stairs was Lavender Dock, which was one of James Small Sedger's properties in 1843. It was later occupied by William Walker, who built there some composite tea clippers (that is, of wood and iron), including the 824-ton *Lothair* of 1870, which was named after the hero of a novel by the Prime Minister, Benjamin Disraeli. She was one of the finest of her class.

Immediately downstream of Lavender Dock there stood in 1843 the premises of Thomas and William Beech, shipbreakers. This firm afterwards moved to Low Globe Dock, where *H.M.S. Queen*, a 110-gun, first-rate ship of the line, was broken up in 1870. The firm seemed to act as an agent for Castle's of Millbank. They occupied Beatson's yard in 1858, when Henry Castle bought it after John Beatson's death. John Beatson had married Sarah Ann, the daughter of William Punnett, whose firm had occupied the yard near Pageant Stairs before Thomas and William Beech.

The next yard was well downstream, past Pageant Stairs and Cuckold's Point, and into Limehouse Reach. This was Nelson Dock, significant remains of whose shipbuilding and ship-repairing days survive amidst the premises of the Holiday Inn Hotel. The yard belonged to a long succession of firms, including John Taylor in the late 17th and early 18th centuries, Randall and Brent (in its various phases) from at least 1756 to 1821, and Bilbe and Perry in the mid-19th century. In the late 1800s it came into the hands of Mills and Knight Ltd., ship repairers, who kept it until 1960. Even at so late a date, however, the yard's career was not over. A firm called Rye-Arc Ltd. bought it and ran it until 1968. Stuart Rankin published a detailed booklet on the yard's history in 1996 (see the bibliography). Nelson Dock was where the *Rising Star* was built in 1821 for the Earl of Dundonald. This vessel is claimed as the second steam warship to be built, which shows that Rotherhithe's yards were not slow to develop new ideas. Just a year later, in fact, another yard, probably near the Greenland Dock, assembled the *Aaron Manby*, a pioneering (but not the first) iron steamship. Incredibly, the vessel had been built in Staffordshire, at the Horseley Works, Tipton. It was subsequently used as a river ferry in France. Another pioneering steamship, the *Kent*, was built in the 1790s by Marmaduke Stalkartt at Nelson Dock. It was built in association with the Society for the Improvement of Naval Architecture, many of whose leaders were influential figures of the time. Stalkartt also built a group of fast Post Office packets.

Of the three yards near the Greenland Dock, two (on either side of Greenland Lock) have been mentioned under Randall and Brent. The third was a very important yard, that of the Wells family, managers and later owners of Greenland Dock itself. It built warships, including 74-gun third-rates, and East Indiamen between 1703 and 1798, when it closed. The yard was located opposite Holy Trinity Church at the eastern end of Rotherhithe Street. It is probable, in fact, that the road turns inland at that point because of the former shipyard.

Finally, mention must be made of that mighty shipbuilding firm, Harland and Wolff of Belfast, which occupied premises at Finland Yard in the Surrey Docks. There they acted as contractors to the Port of London Authority. One of the more extraordinary jobs undertaken in that capacity was to repair Westminster Pier in 1926-7, after the whole pier had been towed downstream to Greenland Dock in November, 1926.

6. Riverside Wharves and Industries

Whereas the Surrey Docks have received much attention over the years, the riverside wharves have rarely been discussed by writers. This is true throughout the Port of London. The wharves certainly formed an important part of Rotherhithe's economy, which was only partly related to the work of the Surrey Docks. 'Wharf' was always a flexible term. It could mean an open quayside or (more usually) a warehouse of at least three or four storeys, each of the storeys having an opening called a loophole on both the riverside and the landside. A warehouse might be used merely for storage, or it could be a mill or a factory for one of a wide range of trades. A few examples will illustrate the variety. Sunderland Wharf was used from 1903 by British Oil and Cake Mills Ltd. to produce oil by crushing seeds; Clarence Wharf traded in stone and polished marble; and King's Mills Wharf was used in 1857 to store tar and turpentine. Uses varied over time and tended to involve bigger businesses (and premises) the later the date.

The timber trade was most evident in Limehouse Reach. Two major wharves north of Commercial Dock Pier, Trinity Wharf and Durand's Wharf, had extensive river frontages which were devoted to handling timber. Trinity Wharf had substantial sheds, whereas its neighbour offered a large open quayside, criss-crossed with the tracks for a travelling crane, which went across Rotherhithe Street to another property adjoining Acorn Pond. The library has various 19th-century deeds for Trinity Wharf. One records that Thomas Oldfield, described as a ship owner of Rotherhithe, bought the property from the Duke of Bedford in 1800 for £2,550. It is interesting to note that when he died in 1807, his will made bequests not only to his family but also to William Ritchie, who had bought the Greenland Dock the year before, and to two boat builders. Subsequently, the property was in the hands of wine merchants, 'dealers in rums, brandies and other spiritous liquors', and beer merchants. The first definite datable link with the timber trade was in 1896, when John Holloway was the occupier; a plan of his property shows a large timber jetty. The following year, he leased the wharf to the Metropolitan Firewood Co. Ltd. The one wharf farther upstream which was consistently involved in the timber trade was Canada Wharf, adjoining the Blacksmiths' Arms public house and near Lavender Lock. A sale catalogue of 1858 mentions newly-erected sawing and planing mills, a new 40 h.p. double-cylinder steam engine, and a bonded timber yard across Rotherhithe Street. As if the timber storage in the wharves and in the docks was not enough, timber was also floated in the river off Trinity and Durand's Wharves. Men called 'rafters' used to lash the timbers together with ropes and heavy iron staples. This was a skilled job, because it was important to secure the timber in the face of the river's strong current.

It was stated in the previous chapter that the trade in grain handled in the docks was substantial, but subsidiary to the trade in timber. An overall view of the wharves would reverse those positions. In the Port of London Authority's photographs of riverside premises in 1937, which were published in 1987 as **London's Lost Riverscape**, the tell-tale white stain down the stack of loopholes appears on many a wharf to indicate its use as a granary. The King and Queen Granary, erected in 1822 immediately downstream of Bull Head Dock, was a massive structure, seven floors high and with its own dock for barges placed under it. In 1857, **Loveday's Waterside Surveys** stated that 'it is, in fact, the best granary represented in this work, and probably the best in England'. The parochial valuation of 1843 attributed to it a gross rent of £1,602, in contrast to Bull Head Dock's £483. The granary was later rebuilt as part of the premises of Bellamy's Wharf and Dock Co. Ltd. and was a leading establishment in the handling of bulk grain. In front of it earlier this century there was an impressive jetty, 350 ft. long, which offered facilities for large ships equal to the best of any upriver wharf.

Globe Wharf, immediately upstream of Globe Stairs, was once an even bigger granary than the King and Queen Wharf of 1822, for in 1887 it could hold 60,000 quarters of corn, against the other building's 50,000. (A quarter is eight bushels or 64 gallons by capacity.) Globe Wharf was later used for the storage and milling of rice.

The grain trade was particularly prominent on the riverfront upstream of Church Stairs. Between there and King's Stairs, Loveday lists seven substantial granaries. The Thames Tunnel Mills were prominent earlier this century in the hands of White, Tomkins and Courage, who milled

Rotherhithe Street, at the junction with Beatson Street, 1929. The Three Compasses is on the right and Globe Wharf is on the left.

rice and maize. Hope Granary, from St. Marychurch Street, has become well-known in recent years as Hope Sufferance Wharf. 'Sufferance' referred to the permission from H.M. Customs to store dutiable goods in places other than the original designated quays in the Upper Pool. East India Wharf was a granary run by the well-known firm of John Dudin & Sons in the late 19th century. Price's Wharf and Gordon's Wharf, just upstream of Elephant Stairs, were run for many decades by Gillman and Spencer. The tall chimney of their mill was a landmark near St. Mary's Church.

An industry on the Rotherhithe waterfront in days past which was dependent on the grain trade was the manufacture of what were called 'sea-biscuits', that is, the rather hard biscuits for the use of the Royal Navy and of merchant ships which were once standard issue. A newspaper cutting of 1741 refers to the building at Rotherhithe of 'five more new ovens for baking biscuit for the use of the Navy', making nine in all. These ovens were associated with the King's Mills, which stand out on early maps, for the mill stream ran across otherwise empty land in the middle of the peninsula, where the Surrey Docks were later built. In 1857, the mills were largely occupied by the firm of Messrs. R. and F. Mangles, wharfingers and millers, but the downstream portion of the site was still a sea-biscuit bakery, run by Messrs. H. Powell & Sons. There were then eight ovens, each with a chimney, within a three-storey building which had a 16 h.p. engine driven by two wrought-iron, low-pressure steam boilers. The bakery was on the south side of Rotherhithe Street and was connected by a bridge to a riverside warehouse.

There was one other significant watermill in Rotherhithe: the Surrey Mill near the junction of West Lane and Rotherhithe Street. This was the mill whose mill stream ran along Southwark Park Road and gave rise to the 'seven islands'. In 1843 it was in the hands of James Robert Mangles and was recorded as having the high rental of £742. Between Hawkstone Road and Rotherhithe New Road there was the district's only windmill, known as the Manor Mill. It was leased by Richard and Joseph Leftwich in the early 19th century.

Barge-building and barge-repairing were important at Rotherhithe long after shipbuilding had ceased. In the short stretch of riverfront between Rotherhithe Stairs and Elephant Stairs, the firms of Henry Pocock, George Pace, and Braithwaite & Dean occupied much property well into this century. The surviving riverside house, 1 Fulford Street, belonged for many years to Braithwaite & Dean. Prewar photographs of this part of the riverfront always show a considerable number of barges. Farther downstream there was until 1997 the well-known firm of Charles Hay & Son. This firm was set up by Francis Theodore Hay (died 1838), the proprietor of Hay's Wharf in Southwark, for his son, Charles, who preferred barge-building to wharfingering. Francis Theodore Hay is buried at St. Mary's, near its tower. Further barge-building firms of note were Talbot Brothers, with no fewer than five addresses in Rotherhithe Street, and Perkins & Homer Ltd. of Dantzig Wharf next to Nelson Dock.

The stretch of riverfront from King's Stairs to Elephant Stairs encompassed in 1857 the premises of four mastmakers, one sailmaker and two ship's blockmakers. Such small-scale businesses devoted to the needs of shipping were typical of that quarter in the days of sail. Associated with them were the ropemakers, who worked inland because of the need of space for their ropewalks. The library has deeds of one ropewalk which was sited between Rotherhithe New Road and Southwark Park Road.

The gas industry on Rotherhithe's riverfront began when the Surrey Consumers' Gas Co. set up their works just upstream of the King's Mills. The site was taken over by the South Metropolitan Gas Co. in 1879 and eventually extended to six and a half acres, including a frontage to the Lower Pool. Coal was supplied in the Thames tradition of 'sea-coal' from the north-east of England. After the Second World War a jetty 200 ft. long was used to moor colliers which could carry up to 2,500 tons of coal. The **S.S. Brixton** was built for the task at Newcastle-upon-Tyne in 1946. Four cranes were provided at the jetty, each of which could unload up to 75 tons of coal an hour. It would take ten to twelve hours to unload an entire collier. The works had a capacity of 9.6 million cubic feet a day after the Second World War. The main gasholder in use in that period, labelled No.3, had been built in 1935 and could hold 800,000 cubic feet. No.4 (of 1932) could hold only 18,000 cubic feet. Nos. 1 and 2, which dated from the 1860s and could hold 1,600,000 cubic feet between them, were put out of action by bombing. Gas production ceased at Rotherhithe in 1959, but a gasholder remains.

The South Metropolitan Gas Co. was one of the most enlightened industrial employers in south London. At Rotherhithe it built housing for some of its workers. Seven houses were erected in Brunel Road in 1926 and were replaced after bombing. In 1931 a more ambitious scheme was carried through in Moodkee Street, half a mile from the works: the building of three blocks of flats named Murdock, Clegg and Neptune Houses, totalling 30 flats.

Coal was delivered to various wharves as well as to the gas works. The second building on the riverfront from the Bermondsey boundary was Naylor's Coal Wharf, established in 1838 and rebuilt at great expense in 1868. A contemporary view of the new wharf bears this description: 'The top storey... is divided into immense hoppers, capable of containing 3,000 tons, where coals are stored direct from the ships, moored abreast of the wharf. The coals are lifted by means of hydraulic cranes, and are transferred to the several hoppers allotted to them, from whence they are drawn off through screens and are weighed whilst running from the mouth of the hopper into sacks, the small running through the screens into the lower hoppers, so that the coals cannot fail to be thoroughly screened, and free from small'. A little way downstream, Hope Coal Wharf operated on similar lines.

The production of power at Rotherhithe was not limited to gas. The London Hydraulic Power Co. built a pumping station in Renforth Street in 1902, next to the Surrey Docks. The converted buildings remain today, dominated by a tall chimney. The heyday of hydraulic power in London was between the wars. The mains went westwards from the station towards Bermondsey and also across the river through the Rotherhithe Tunnel. The company ceased operations completely in 1977. Hydraulic power was used for such things as cranes and lifts.

The historic heart of Rotherhithe, 1926. Rotherhithe Gas Works is on the right. The chimney on the left belongs to the London Hydraulic Power Co's pumping station.

On many maps over a long period, one factory near Lower Road stands out: the business known as Brandram's. It stands out partly because it was a notably large concern, and partly because it was already sited there when all the surrounding land was still open pasture. In its last years – the works closed in 1958 – the firm was known as Brandram Brothers & Co. Ltd. and occupied a site between the bend of Neptune Street and Canada Dock. The firm manufactured white lead and paint, and refined saltpetre and flowers of sulphur. In 1882, 90 men were said to be employed in producing lead. The parochial valuation of 1843 distinguishes between the old factory and the new premises to its north. Both sites remained in use until 1958. Samuel Brandram redeemed the land tax on no fewer than five acres in 1800, when the premises were cited as an oil of vitriol manufactory.

Another lead factory of note at Rotherhithe was the one belonging to H.T. Enthoven & Sons at Upper Ordnance Wharf. Lead, tin and antimony were produced there. The factory closed in 1980.

The last industry to be considered is an unexpected one: the production of manure. In 1857, when Bull Head Dock was still occupied by shipwrights, it was flanked upstream by William Caudery, guano merchant and manure manufacturer, and downstream by Messrs. Mellersh and Jolliffe, chemical manure manufacturers. Such establishments were to be found inland, too. In 1861-2 one Horatio John Salmon ran Salmon's Manure Works in Galleywall Road. The Vestry's annual reports in the later 19th century refer to many complaints about the smells of manure and similar substances. In 1890, mention was made of an extraordinary case in Suffolk Street, off Rotherhithe New Road, in which 'the stench was such as issues from stored fish offal when it has become putrid'. 'This vile stuff', the report continues, '... was actually being mixed with lime to form plaster for the houses'. As the old saying had it, 'where there's muck, there's brass'!

7. Tunnels Under The Thames

In the 19th century the profession of civil engineer attracted much public esteem and prestige, and of all its practitioners none was more famous than Isambard Kingdom Brunel (1806-1859). At Rotherhithe he worked with his father, Sir Marc Brunel (1769-1849), in the building of the Thames Tunnel, which was the first completed underwater tunnel in the world. For this remarkable pioneering work, Sir Marc had invented a tunnelling shield, which was prompted by his observations of the *teredo navalis* or shipworm. Never before had a full-sized tunnel been driven through water-bearing ground, and the success of Sir Marc's method provided the basis for all subsequent examples, including the Channel Tunnel of our own day. The only previous attempt of note to tunnel under the Thames had also taken place at Rotherhithe. In 1807-8, two Cornish mining engineers, Robert Vazie and Richard Trevithick, excavated a driftway or small pilot tunnel for the Thames Archway Co., but lack of money led to its abandonment before completion.

The Thames Tunnel was authorised by an Act of Parliament in 1824. One of its most influential supporters was the Duke of Wellington. Work began in March, 1825, when a shaft 42 ft. in diameter was sunk at Rotherhithe. Tunnelling then began from that end, using a shield which was built for Sir Marc by Henry Maudslay, another famous figure in 19th-century engineering. William Armstrong was the original resident engineer, but he resigned in 1826. Isambard Kingdom Brunel succeeded him, aged just twenty, and he went to live at Cow Court, which is now represented by Tunnel Road, to the east of St. Mary's Church. Irruptions of water threatened the work from time to time. On five occasions the danger was severe, the worst incident occurring on January 12th, 1828, when six men were drowned. When a major irruption took place, a diving bell was used to identify the hole in the river-bed, and clay was then applied in prodigious quantities to stop it up. The tunnel was next pumped dry, and tunnelling resumed. Later in 1828, however, work was suspended completely for want of money: a common circumstance in major, pioneering projects. The middle of the river had been reached when tunnelling stopped. A brick wall was built across the tunnelling end, and a large mirror was mounted on it, in order to give the illusion of a continuous archway to the numerous visitors. For seven years the admission of visitors was the only activity on the site.

Work was resumed in 1835 after a loan had been secured from the Treasury. A new tunnelling shield had to be made, and this time it was supplied by Rennie Bros., the firm headed by Sir John Rennie, who had lately built London Bridge to his father's designs. Tunnelling was completed as far as the Wapping shaft on November 16th, 1841, and then the whole tunnel had to be tiled, paved and otherwise finished. The final result consisted of two arched passages 1,200 ft. long between Rotherhithe and Wapping. Each passage is 14 ft. wide and 16½ ft. high and is divided from the other by a wall 4 ft. thick, punctuated with 64 arched openings. The head of each passage is 16 ft. below the bed of the Thames. The tunnel was formally opened on March 25th, 1843. It had cost about £600,000.

Access was provided for pedestrians by huge, circular staircases. The tunnel attracted large numbers of people, as much out of curiosity as for routine use. In the week ending November 16th, 1858, for example, no fewer than 19,492 pedestrians passed through, paying a total of £81 4s 4d. The tunnel also witnessed dinners, concerts and other special events. It had always been intended to build spiral carriage ramps, 40 ft. in width, but lack of money baulked the plan. This deficiency was fatal to the commercial value of the tunnel. The lack of wheeled traffic torpedoed its promoters' hopes. In 1865 the whole thing was sold to the East London Railway Co. for £200,000 and was adapted for the use which it retains today, as part of the Underground railway system.

The East London Railway Co. was incorporated in 1865 and was intended to link the Great Eastern Railway with Brighton and the south-east of England. The company's line through the Thames Tunnel was opened on December 7th, 1869, from Whitechapel to New Cross Gate. A station was opened at Rotherhithe in Adam Street; this street was renamed Brunel Road in 1905. The next station down the line (and the only other one within Rotherhithe) was originally named Deptford Road. It was renamed Surrey Docks Station on July 17th, 1911. More recently, there has come a further, and markedly unpopular, change to Surrey Quays.

Two years after the railway's opening, the line was extended to Shoreditch to provide a connection with the Great Eastern Railway at Liverpool Street

Station. The London, Brighton and South Coast Railway subsequently ran a service from Liverpool Street to Croydon, and between 1876 and 1884 there were some through trains from Liverpool Street to Brighton. It was surely very odd indeed for trains to the south coast to start from a north-facing station north of the river. From 1884 the Metropolitan Railway ran services to New Cross after a link had been built between Aldgate and Whitechapel Stations, but the firm did not have exclusive use of the line. In 1913 the route was electrified, and then all the trains were those of the Metropolitan Railway. For much of this century the services have been purely local ones, running between Whitechapel and New Cross, but long-distance trains through the tunnel played a valuable part during the two world wars. The Duke of Wellington, who supported Sir Marc Brunel's original scheme because he saw its strategic value, would have been gratified.

The Thames Tunnel was the first tunnel under the Thames; its neighbour, the Rotherhithe Tunnel, was the thirteenth. It is not surprising, therefore, that whereas the pioneering scheme took eighteen years to build, the later one took just four, between 1904 and 1908. It was built for the London County Council to the plans of Maurice Fitzmaurice of Messrs. Price and Reeves. He was also the chief engineer of the Woolwich Foot Tunnel. The London County Council decided to go ahead with a tunnel at Rotherhithe in 1899, and secured parliamentary approval through the Thames Tunnel (Rotherhithe and Ratcliff) Act of 1900. Work on the tunnel proper did not start until 1904, but much effort was expended long before that on what the London County Council called 'displacement dwellings'. The council had concluded that up to 1,500 people would lose their homes when the southern approach to the tunnel was built. A site was acquired in Swan Road (between Brunel Road and the river), on which large blocks of tenements were built. Winchelsea Buildings were finished in 1902, and Rye Buildings and Sandwich Buildings followed in 1903. Hythe Buildings and Seaford Buildings completed the estate. These all survive today and rank as the oldest municipal housing in Rotherhithe. Out of the total cost of Rotherhithe Tunnel of over £2 million, one half was the cost of acquiring property for the approaches and of rehousing those who were displaced.

The tunnelling itself was complete by August, 1907, and the whole project was opened on June 12th, 1908, by the Prince of Wales (later King George V). E.H. Tabor had been the resident engineer in charge of construction and it was clearly to his credit that no irruption of water or serious injury to the workmen had occurred. The Southwark Local Studies Library possesses a well-illustrated volume which he compiled about the building of the tunnel. No set of illustrations could be more complete for a major work of engineering. Whereas the Thames Tunnel consists of two adjoining passages, the Rotherhithe Tunnel is a single tube, the inside of which has a diameter of 27 ft. The tube is made up of cast-iron rings, each 2½ ft. wide and weighing 19 tons. The cast-iron tunnel is 1,212 yds. or 3,636 ft. long. The approaches almost double that distance to 6,883 ft. or about one and a third miles. These approaches have a gradient of about 1 in 36 and have at each entrance a gauge arch, made up of a tunnelling shield's cutting edge.

The Rotherhithe approach runs parallel with Brunel Road and Albion Street, and crosses the line of the Thames Tunnel almost at right angles. The approach road altered the street pattern, so that, for example, Neptune Street was cut in half. The southern end was left as Neptune Street, but the northern end, which includes the Neptune public house, was renamed Rupack Street.

A scheme to renovate Rotherhithe Tunnel was approved by the Greater London Council in 1979. The work took eight months to undertake and the tunnel was reopened in April, 1981. Back in 1963 there had been a plan to introduce one-way working, north to south, but opposition halted it, despite the favour of the then Bermondsey Borough Council.

One of the places of interest in Rotherhithe today is Sir Marc Brunel's engine house, in Railway Avenue, just east of St. Mary's Church. It was built to house boilers, which supplied the power to drain the Thames Tunnel. It now contains a compound horizontal V steam pumping engine, built by J. and G. Rennie of Southwark in 1885, and a detailed display on the history of Sir Marc's tunnel. Next to the engine house there stands a shaft, 80 ft. in diameter, which was used as a pedestrian staircase to the tunnel between 1843 and 1869. The engine house is a valuable and proud reminder of Rotherhithe's and Southwark's significant place in the history of British engineering.

The entrance to Rotherhithe Tunnel, 1909. The gauge arch had been a cutting edge of a tunnelling shield.

8. Municipal Rotherhithe

The local council of Rotherhithe down to 1900 was known as the Vestry, which ruled the civil parish of St. Mary. Local government was arranged by county and by parish, and at the parochial level there was no distinction between the civil and the ecclesiastical until Victorian times. The Rector chaired the Vestry, and the churchwardens were considered to be its most senior officers. It is not surprising, therefore, that Rotherhithe Vestry's constitution was ordained by the Chancellor of the Diocese of Winchester, in 1673. The preamble stated that Rotherhithe's affairs 'have not bin so well carried and ordered as the better and grander sort of the said parishioners have desired and wished'. There was henceforth to be 'an Assembly of the Chiefest of the parish to ye number of 24 besides ye Minister who is alwayes to be reckoned as one of the vestry'. It is remarkable how many of the 'chiefest of the parish' at that time were ships' masters or were otherwise connected with the sea. In 1679, for example, Captain Peter Blake was a collector of the poor rate, Captain Smith was an auditor and one Joseph Ball, mariner, was a sidesman. In the following year Captain John Falstaffe served as overseer of the poor and Captain Matthew Crover as an auditor. A Mr. Buggins took his turn as churchwarden in 1697.

The work of the Vestry in the 17th and 18th centuries largely concerned the church and churchyard, and the Poor Law. There were regular moves to have the churchyard extended. In 1767, for example, the Bishop of Winchester was to be asked to consecrate an additional burial ground. Fees for burials were important in the parochial finances. In 1816-17, the sum of £209 16s 2d was raised from them, out of a total income of £1,579 0s 4d for all matters except the Poor Law. The greater part of this total came from a church rate, which was levied compulsorily on all parishioners before 1868, whether they supported the Church of England or not. The Poor Law gave the parish the most work, for it included the running of the workhouse (see chapter 9) and frequently involved the removal of paupers to other parishes, or appeals to Quarter Sessions for Surrey. These duties, and the flavour of the period, are reflected in this entry in the churchwardens' accounts: 'May 19th 1817. Paid for Chaise hire, Turnpikes and Ostlers. £7 17s 0d'. In 1778 the Vestry Clerk was paid a mere £12 a year. This sum compares with six guineas (£6.30) which were paid in the same year for a greatcoat for the parochial beadle (Rotherhithe's Mr. Bumble). Two years later a gold-laced hat was also bought for him.

The Poor Law was eventually removed from the parish's control, as recounted in chapter 9. The parish was given new responsibilities and renewed life as a unit of local government, however, by the Metropolis Local Management Act of 1855. This Act made considerable changes to London's government. A body called the Metropolitan Board of Works was set up to oversee London-wide matters such as main drainage. The old parishes were largely assimilated to the role of subsidiary authorities to this board. Rotherhithe Vestry therefore had the rank of a district board of works from 1856 to 1900. In 1889 the Metropolitan Board of Works was replaced by the London County Council and in 1900 the parishes were superseded by the metropolitan boroughs. From that date Rotherhithe was part of the Metropolitan Borough of Bermondsey, whose town hall was in Spa Road.

The Metropolitan Board of Works, the London County Council and Rotherhithe Vestry were responsible in Victorian and Edwardian times for founding most of Rotherhithe's municipal institutions: Southwark Park, Rotherhithe Baths, the public library, the town hall and the local fire stations. The park was laid out by the Metropolitan Board of Works on land which had been bought from Sir William Gomm. The fire stations were built by the board and by its successor, the London County Council. The remaining institutions were the work of the Vestry and its offshoots.

An Act of Parliament was passed in 1864 to authorise the Metropolitan Board of Works to buy land at Rotherhithe for a new public park. Some 63 acres were acquired in the following year. Down to March 25th, 1869, a total of £95,162 was spent on the site, mostly on acquisition rather than on laying it out. The formal opening took place on June 19th, 1869. The name refers to the fact that the park fell within the parliamentary constituency of Southwark, although it was wholly in the parish of Rotherhithe. The town of Southwark lay well to the west, beyond Bermondsey. It was a strange decision, but one which was paralleled by the use of a Southwark parochial name, St. Olave's, for the local hospital. In 1921-2, the local Member of Parliament, John Lort Williams, tried to have the name changed to Rotherhithe Park, but the London County Council rejected the idea. The two big features of the park in the early part of last century were the boating lake and the cricket ground. The lake was an addition to the original layout – it was built in 1885 and extended in 1908 – and was an extensive feature in the centre of the park, far bigger than the later pond. The cricket ground, sited towards Hawkstone Road, was known as the Oval as much as the more famous ground at Kennington. It was in Southwark Park that a celebrated Victorian cricketer, Rotherhithe-born Robert Abel ('The Guv'nor'), learnt his skills as a member of the Southwark Park Cricket Club. The improvements of recent years have done much to restore the park to what it was in its Edwardian heyday.

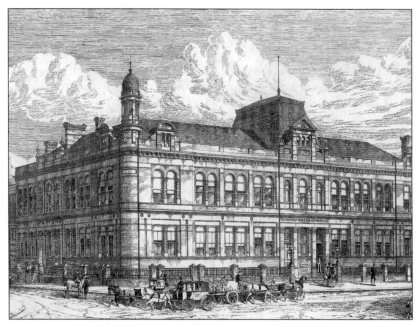

Rotherhithe Baths and Washhouses, Lower Road, 1881.

Rotherhithe Baths were built at the corner of Lower Road and Gomm Road in 1880-1, on the site of a property called Augusta Lodge. Mrs. Carr-Gomm presented the freehold to the parish in 1887. George Elkington & Son designed the original baths' building, which was set up by commissioners on behalf of the parish. There were two substantial swimming baths, but of equal (possibly greater) interest to the local population were the 65 private or 'slipper' baths and the 24 compartments in the washhouse or laundry. These facilities were in popular demand well into the 20th century and remained open after the swimming baths had been put out of use by bombing in the Second World War. Bermondsey Borough Council began the rebuilding of the baths in the early 1960s as its last major project. A plaque was unveiled in the new, but unfinished, building on March 23rd, 1965, to make sure that Bermondsey Borough Council's role would be remembered. The formal opening took place on November 27th, 1965, when the London Borough of Southwark had come into existence. W.S.A. Williams was the architect of the building, whose white textured concrete and stark, unadorned lines were far removed from the stately classicism of its predecessor.

Canon Beck laid the foundation stone of Rotherhithe's first public library on October 23rd, 1889, at 120 Lower Road. The building was opened on October 4th, 1890. The architects were Stock, Page & Stock, and the total cost was a mere £2,800. The library itself was at the back of the site, facing Southwark Park; at the front, on the busy Lower Road, was the librarian's lodging, for in those days the librarian was expected to live at his library. The job went first to one William Marillier (from 1890 to 1895), who had previously been the proprietor and headmaster of Rotherhithe Grammar School at 18 Lower Road. He resigned because of poor health and was succeeded by Herbert Archer Shuttleworth from Birmingham. In 1895-6 he had 2,565 borrowers. They were counted by occupation in the library's annual report. One might expect such entries as eight barge builders, seven lightermen, six shipwrights and three oar makers, but there were no fewer than 39 millstone makers and a stupendous 202 clerks, plus the more curious entry for four detectives. In 1896 a branch was opened in Rotherhithe Street, known as the 'Lower Rotherhithe Delivery Station', for 'the Commissioners were desirous of providing for the intellectual necessities of this district' .

In 1905, as a result of Rotherhithe Town Hall's supersession by the one in Spa Road, the library was moved into that grand building from 120 Lower Road. It remained there until the Second World War. Strictly speaking, it should be referred to there as the Rotherhithe Public Library *and Museum*, for it housed an interesting collection of local portraits, objects and documents. For many years the library was run in that building by Leonard Hobbs, who wrote about the district's history from time to time. In the Second World War there came disaster, for the building was badly damaged in the Blitz and was finally destroyed by a flying bomb in 1944. Temporary accommodation was found in a former Salvation Army hall at 18 Lower Road, which had coincidentally been the site of the Rotherhithe Grammar School, from which Rotherhithe's first librarian came in 1890. The temporary home lasted for 30 years, for not until October, 1975, was a new, purpose-built library opened, in Albion Street, behind the Norwegian church. Yorke, Rosenberg & Mardall were the architects, and it had space for 17,000 books. It cannot be called architecturally handsome, in the manner of its prewar predecessor, but it fulfils a worthy role in providing a popular service which is now more than a century old in the district.

Rotherhithe Town Hall was opened on April 28th, 1897, only three years before Rotherhithe Vestry ceased to be the local authority. The Vestry had previously met in the baths' building. The erection of a substantial town hall was a prominent example of Victorian civic pride. It is a great pity that the building was destroyed by bombing, for it was a handsome structure and was adorned with much well-executed sculpture. It was arguably the grandest building ever erected in the district. The design of Messrs. Murray & Foster was chosen in 1894, and the foundation stone was laid on September 17th, 1895. Red brick and Portland stone were the principal materials. There was a frontage of $52\frac{1}{2}$ ft. to Lower Road, opposite St. Olave's Hospital; the side elevation to Neptune Street extended for 161 ft. and occupied the whole block back to Moodkee Street. This elevation had numerous bands of stone, divided by red brick, producing the appearance of streaky bacon which many Victorian buildings effected.

The meeting hall of the Vestry was placed on the first floor at the front, above the Vestry's offices, and was accessible from the main entrance. This doorway was distinguished by the caryatids or Greek female figures which acted the part of flanking columns; Henry Poole was the sculptor. A public hall to seat 891 people was provided at the back of the building and was entered from Moodkee Street.

The opening ceremony was attended by the band of the 3rd Volunteer Battalion of the Royal West Surrey Regiment, commanded by Colonel S.B. Bevington; one of the battalion's drill halls had formerly stood on the site.

Two fire stations were built at Rotherhithe. The first was put up in Gomm Road (behind the baths' site) by the Metropolitan Board of Works. The other was opened in 1903 at Pageant's Wharf in Rotherhithe Street. It was noted at the time that a steam fire engine had been provided, 'in view of the fact that the water supply in this neighbourhood is poor'. The water pipe in Rotherhithe Street was apparently of small diameter. Both stations went out of use long ago. The site of the one in Gomm Road was taken for the new baths in the 1960s. The building in Rotherhithe Street still stands.

No chapter on local government in Rotherhithe can fail to make reference to municipal housing, which loomed so large in the 20th century. It is very largely a story of the 1930s and of the 1950s and 1960s. The first scheme, however, goes back to the days of the Vestry in 1896, when a plan was drawn up to replace slum housing in Braddon Street and Fulford Street, near King's Stairs. Under Part II of the Housing of the Working Classes Act, a Victorian measure, half the cost could be sought from the London County Council. In the event, the foundation stone of the scheme was not laid until October 31st, 1903, and the four blocks of tenements were finished only in 1904 and 1905. Messrs. Brocklesby, Marchant & East were the architects. These blocks were finished after the London County Council's own blocks in Swan Road, which were built in association with the Rotherhithe Tunnel (see chapter 7); the Swan Road properties were therefore the first completed council dwellings in Rotherhithe.

The Bermondsey Borough Council was responsible for the major building campaign of the 1920s and the 1930s. The Labour majority on the Council from 1922 determined to replace as many of the decayed 18th- and 19th-century houses as possible. The Amos Estate, Lavender House, the Silver Walk Estate, the Acorn Walk Estate and the Redriff Estate considerably altered the appearance of much of Rotherhithe Street in those years. On the western side of Rotherhithe there were built in the same era the Adams Gardens Estate between Brunel Road and St. Marychurch Street; the Millpond Estate near West Lane; and the Kirby Estate on the corner of Jamaica Road and Southwark Park Road. After the Second World War, much Council housing was built along Southwark Park Road and Rotherhithe New Road. The most noticeable postwar estate, however, was the Canada Estate, built by the London County Council in the early 1960s on the site of Brandram's works. Most of the flats were provided in two 21- storey blocks which were among the least graceful of postwar towers and which stand out painfully from as far away as London Bridge, when looking downstream.

9. St. Olave's Hospital

For about a century Rotherhithe had its own general hospital in Lower Road, which was known in its later decades as St. Olave's Hospital. It grew out of the infirmary of Rotherhithe Workhouse, which was run by the St. Olave's Poor Law Union in the late 19th century. The emergence of modern hospitals from Poor Law institutions was widespread in England. Lambeth Hospital, Dulwich Hospital, St. Francis's Hospital (at East Dulwich) and St. Giles's Hospital (at Camberwell) were further local examples of the pattern.

Rotherhithe Workhouse, Lower Road, 1826, from a watercolour by George Yates.

The Poor Law in England went back to the reign of Queen Elizabeth I, but it was only in the 1720s that the parish of Rotherhithe set up a workhouse. Poor relief before that date was outdoor relief, that is, it consisted of payments to individuals who remained in their own homes. The first proposal in the parish to establish a workhouse was recorded in the Vestry Minutes of April 29th, 1722. Rules were drawn up for the running of the establishment. Nothing was done, however, for six years. The proposal was revived in May, 1728, and on that occasion action was taken. A workhouse was built in Lower Road, opposite what is now the junction with Neptune Street, on a site which was then outside the built-up area of Rotherhithe. Until 1836 it came under the control of the parish of Rotherhithe as represented by its Vestry. A watercolour of it in the 1820s is held in Southwark Local Studies Library: a neat building with a long road frontage, and certainly not reminiscent of the 'Bastilles' against which Charles Dickens railed. Life within its walls, however, had its share of grimness. Four girls who were inmates in 1835 were threatened with banishment to Van Diemen's Land (Tasmania in Australia) for bad conduct. Eleven years later it was decided that unclaimed paupers' bodies would be sent for dissection, which was the same fate that executed criminals had long faced. Then there is the minute of 1840, by which an irritated Vestry decided to offer a reward of £5 for information about an infant who had been abandoned on the workhouse steps. This was a real-life case at Rotherhithe of an Oliver Twist, three years after Victoria became Queen.

From 1839 until 1869 the workhouse was placed under the Rotherhithe Board of Guardians, which was a purely local body and which shared many members with the Vestry, although it was strictly separate. It was also much regulated by the Poor Law Board, a department of the central government, whereas the old parish had been subject only to the decisions of the Quarter Sessions for Surrey, and they were little more than arbitrations in disputes. After 1869 Rotherhithe was part of St. Olave's Union, which took its name from St. Olave's Church near London Bridge. Poor Law Unions were encouraged by the Poor Law Amendment Act of 1834. It was considered more economical to join parishes together for the purposes of Poor relief and to build large workhouses for the unions so created. These workhouses were Dickens's 'Bastilles'. The Act also aimed to do away with outdoor relief and to limit poor relief to workhouses, and to make them 'less eligible' or so ghastly that only the genuinely destitute would stomach them. In Rotherhithe (and elsewhere in the present London Borough of Southwark) there was little diminution of outdoor relief, or more prominence for the workhouse. What undoubtedly did change was the intervention of central government. By the 1860s the local board of guardians was receiving regular orders from Whitehall, whereas half a century earlier the parish made its own decisions about poor relief.

St. Olave's Union, which ran the Poor Law in Rotherhithe from 1869 to 1930, initially decided to house able-bodied male paupers at Rotherhithe. Subsequently this decision was rescinded. The workhouse proper was closed permanently on July 29th, 1884. Its infirmary remained, for by an order of August 31st, 1875, it had become the infirmary or Poor Law hospital for the whole union. In 1904 the St. Olave's Union was renamed the Bermondsey Union, and so its hospital became Bermondsey Infirmary. Fifteen years later, application was made to the then new Ministry of Health to change its name to Bermondsey and Rotherhithe Hospital. The further change to St. Olave's Hospital came after the London County Council had assumed responsibility in 1930.

A workhouse was ostensibly an establishment in which paupers were meant to work in return for their board and lodging. At Rotherhithe a workroom was built for this very purpose in 1766. 'Work' in this context would usually be tedious and marginal, and apparently pointless, such as oakum-picking or stone-breaking. Rotherhithe, however, had a more purposive and profitable scheme, at least in the earlier 19th century: a rope manufactory, entirely appropriate to a seafaring parish. In 1836 it made a profit of £592 2s 2d. It must be remembered here that many inmates of a workhouse were not able-bodied. Of the 194 inmates at Rotherhithe on May 18th, 1866, for example, no fewer than 140 were disabled or old or infirm. Nineteen more were children, leaving only 35 able-bodied adults. (The workhouse was then capable of holding 340.)

Medical care of the poor was in the hands of a retained surgeon in the 18th century; 'Lancelot Copplestone, practitioner in physic and chyrurgery' (surgery) was one appointee who was named (with much approbation) in the Vestry Minutes. In 1837 the first Medical Officer for the parish was appointed, at a salary of £120 a year, including medicines. It was estimated that he would see 1,200 patients annually. Thirty years later the Medical Officer accredited to the workhouse was paid only £35 a year, which even the Poor Law Board considered 'miserably low'. The sum contrasted with Bermondsey's £80 and Lambeth's princely £300. Subsequently, the Medical Officer's pay was raised to £50, and two further appointments were made to East and West Districts of the parish at £80 each.

The infirmary of the workhouse in the middle of the 19th century had 50 beds arranged in six wards. By 1866, when the Poor Law Board's inspector reported on the premises, a new infirmary of 52 beds in four wards had been added. This new infirmary had just one paid nurse; the rest were unpaid pauper nurses in the tradition of Sarah Gamp, whom Dickens presented to the world as a representative of a wayward system which needed to be reformed. We know of many deficiencies in Rotherhithe Workhouse's infirmary in the mid-1860s because a paid nurse in 1864-5, Martha Beeton, wrote a long letter of complaint to the Poor Law Board. The board considered that her evidence showed 'an animus which makes it necessary to receive it with caution', but enough of her complaints were upheld to require the departure of the then master and matron of the workhouse.

The St. Olave's Union Infirmary of 1875 was new both in its status and in its buildings. *The Builder* of April 22nd, 1874 reported that work had been in progress for the previous eighteen months on five blocks which would have a combined frontage to Southwark Park of 300 ft. The site was a spacious one at the back of the old workhouse and had the advantage of overlooking the relatively new park. The five blocks, designed by H. Saxon Snell, were built of stock bricks with bands of red Fareham bricks and with ornamental window heads. The infirmary opened on May 24th, 1876. A further report appeared in *The Builder* on April 9th, 1892, concerning alterations and extensions designed by Messrs. Newman and Newman (a local firm of architects). The resultant plan of the infirmary was of the five blocks connected by a long corridor, plus five smaller buildings nearby. A typical Victorian institution was complete.

In the early 20th century, the changing political complexion of the St. Olave's Board of Guardians (which was an elected body) brought pressure for improvements at the infirmary and to dissociate it from the Poor Law as far as possible. A famous local G.P., Dr. Alfred Salter, who was later to become the first Labour Member of Parliament for West Bermondsey, was the leading proponent of improvement on the board. His party's journal, the *Bermondsey Labour Magazine*, stated in 1926 that 'it has been the deliberate policy of the Labour Party to remove from the hospital all taint and stigma of the Poor Law'. By then, the infirmary had been renamed the Bermondsey and Rotherhithe Hospital. Under its Superintendent, Dr. R.C. Harkness, there were six doctors, a matron, four assistant matrons, fourteen ward sisters, one theatre sister, one masseuse and no fewer than 114 nurse-probationers. By that time the hospital offered a training-school for nurses. The days of a single paid nurse and unpaid pauper nurses were long superseded. A general raising of standards was seen to be reflected in patients' diminishing average stay in the hospital from 63 days in 1919 to 35 in 1923 and 27 in 1925. The average at Guy's and St. Thomas's at the time was 21. The total number of admissions in 1925 was 6,063, with 514 in residence on December 31st of that year. Balconies were added to the Victorian ward blocks in 1924 to make them more attractive.

St. Olave's passed from the London County Council to the National Health Service in 1948. The succeeding years might be seen as its heyday. An annual nurses' prizegiving was the occasion for inviting a distinguished guest, which gave the hospital regular publicity. Sir Ralph Richardson came in 1956, Vivien Leigh in 1959; and the local Member of Parliament, Robert Mellish, in 1960. The guest in 1953, Prince Olav of Norway (who became King Olav V of Norway in 1957), left a lasting memento. He gave each nurse a badge bearing an image of St. Olav which had been copied from one in Trondheim Cathedral in Norway. It became the hospital's badge and appeared to contribute much to its sense of identity and pride for some years. Summer fetes also helped in this respect.

At the beginning of the 1960s the hospital had 12 working wards: six for women, five for men and one for children. There were over 200 nurses and more than 300 other staff. The overall annual cost was about £400,000. The subsequent twenty years saw a series of threats to the hospital's survival and eventually witnessed its closure. The first significant threat to close it came in 1963. The difficulty in which the hospital found itself was that it was not an independent institution, which could make its own decisions and strive for an obvious efficiency; it was part of a group, in which the bigger hospitals (especially Guy's) were always going to be safeguarded first. The casualty department in Lower

Road was shut in 1970. In-patients ceased to be admitted in 1979. The final chapter, the closing of the out-patients' section, followed in 1984. Most of the hospital's site was eventually put to use for housing.

10. Schools, Churches and Charities

Rotherhithe's most ancient school is the one founded in 1613 by Peter Hills and Robert Bell. Hills was an eminent mariner, for he was an Elder Brother of Trinity House, and his school was to be for eight sons of mariners from the parish. Various names have attached to the school, because two 18th-century endowments were merged with the original one. 'Free School' was the first title. In the early 18th century, new funds were gathered to support more pupils (65 boys and 50 girls). Finally, in 1739, an Amicable Society was set up with further money, to educate 77 boys. All these endowments were amalgamated in 1849. The original school building was on the north side of St. Marychurch Street, adjoining the church. It was rebuilt there in 1746. Half a century later, in 1795, the sum of £400 was spent on buying a house on the other side of the road from Richard Vidler. This still stands as No. 70 St. Marychurch Street and is the building to whose facade there are affixed Portland stone figures of a charity boy and girl. The building dates from about 1700 and it was therefore almost a century old before it became a school. Girls ceased to be educated there when St. Mary's School in Lower Road opened in 1836. Accommodation for boys was subsequently increased at the old site by building in the garden. About 150 boys were taught there by the end of the 19th century.

On the eastern side of Rotherhithe, another charity school was founded in 1755; it was known as the United Society's School. In 1791 the Duke of Bedford gave a piece of land on the west side of Trinity Street (later part of Rotherhithe Street), where a schoolroom and a house were completed in the following year. The library holds a minute book from this school, which lists candidates for admission, and gives details of their parents. In one year, 1842, there were 33 candidates, of whom one third exactly were the children of shipwrights. A majority of the remainder were from families connected with the river. The school merged in 1875 with the one belonging to Holy Trinity parish.

The foundation of further voluntary schools, and of the churches with which they were associated, was the result of an extraordinary expansion in the Church of England's work in Rotherhithe in the 1830s. The sudden expansion was due to the energy of the Reverend Edward Blick, Rector from 1835 to 1867. In common with many of his contemporaries, he took the view that the Church needed to expand and to be forceful if it was to have the same role in industrial Victorian England that it had exercised in, say, the England of Queen Anne. His contemporary, Charles Blomfield, Bishop of London, set up the Metropolis New Churches Fund to build churches in poor districts. More locally, a Southwark Fund for Schools and Churches was launched in 1845 to work in the crowded riverside areas, including Rotherhithe.

Lower Road, c.1920. St. Mary's School stands on the left. Southwark Park Wesleyan Methodist Church stands prominently in the centre.

St. Mary's Church was the only Anglican place of worship in Rotherhithe until 1838. No fewer than three new churches were then opened within a couple of years, and a fourth followed in 1850. These churches were Holy Trinity, Rotherhithe Street (built in 1837-8 and designed by Sampson Kempthorne); Christ Church at the corner of Jamaica Road and Cathay Street (1838-9, by Lewis Vulliamy); All Saints' in Lower Road, opposite St. Olave's Hospital (1840, by Sampson Kempthorne); and St. Paul's in Beatson Street, off Rotherhithe Street (1850). Sir William Gomm gave the sites for Christ Church and All Saints'; eventually, he and his wife were buried at Christ Church. The site for Holy Trinity Church was given by the Commercial Dock Co. Of the four, only Holy Trinity Church exists today. The present building is Thomas F. Ford's replacement in 1959-60 of the bombed original. All Saints' was also bombed, but was not replaced. St. Paul's and Christ Church were demolished after the war, Christ Church as recently as 1979.

Edward Blick managed the remarkable feat of opening ten new schoolrooms within a dozen years. In 1836 he secured a grant of land in Lower Road from Sir William Gomm to set up St. Mary's School. This was to be the principal school in the parish for many decades. It was for long referred to as 'a national school', that is, a school run in association with the National Society for the Education of the Poor in the Principles of the Established Church, which was founded in 1811 to encourage education within the Church of England. St. Mary's School was sited in Lower Road for nearly a century and a half and was familiar to generations of Rotherhithe folk, because it had a prominent site at the junction with Culling Road, where Lower Road curved away from the tunnel entrance.

Old people's tea in Rotherhithe Great Hall, Lower Road, 1938.

The school run in connection with Holy Trinity Church was inaugurated in 1836 in that part of Rotherhithe Street which was then known as Trinity Street. It was run as a national school and ranked second only to St. Mary's for the number of children educated. In 1875 it took over the work of the United Society's School. It lasted until 1910, when it ceased after the opening nearby of the London County Council's Redriff School. Voluntary church schools (above all, voluntary Nonconformist schools) found it difficult to compete with local authority establishments, the first of which had been set up in Albion Street in 1872.

Edward Blick's successor as Rector, Edward Josselyn Beck, was no less industrious in overseeing an expansion of the Church's work. In his time (1867-1907), three more parish churches and a university mission were established to serve parts of the ancient parish. The new parish churches were St. Barnabas', Plough Way (built in 1870-2 and designed by William Butterfield); St. Katherine's, Eugenia Road (1884-5, by W.O. Milne); and St. Bartholomew's, Barkworth Road (1886-7, by E. Tapnell Allen). The last of these stood across the boundary in Camberwell, but served a parish which was partly carved out of Rotherhithe. The university mission arose from Clare College's ownership of the advowson of St. Mary's. In 1883, at a time when 'settlements' or centres of voluntary social work were attracting much support in the Churches and in the universities, it was decided at Clare College to attempt the 'Christianizing of some spiritually destitute district'. The link with St. Mary's led to the delineation of a mission district south of Southwark Park. The first Missioner was appointed in 1885 and a church was opened in 1886. This was demolished in 1911 and was replaced the following year by a building which came to be known as the Church of the Epiphany, Dilston Grove. Changing social and economic circumstances led to the giving up of the mission district in 1963. A looser link between Clare College and Rotherhithe continues to this day.

All the churches mentioned above belonged to the Church of England. Many more were built by non-Anglican denominations. The Wesleyan Methodists established a chapel in Silver Street (near Nelson Dock) in 1800, which lasted until 1926. The same denomination founded a church in Albion Street in 1806, which split in the middle of the century. One half stayed in Albion Street and built a chapel affiliated to the United Methodist Free Churches; the other half established the Southwark Park Wesleyan Methodist Church in Lower Road in 1874. It is interesting to note that this building was Gothic and had a tower, in keeping with contemporary Anglican churches. Another Methodist group, the Primitive Methodists, had a church in Jamaica Road from 1856. All these Methodist places of worship supported thriving Sunday schools in Victorian times and in the early 20th century. All have now gone.

The Commercial Dock Chapel was an early Nonconformist enterprise in Rotherhithe: it was opened in Derrick Street in 1800 as a 'tabernacle of witness in the wilderness'. Later in the century its congregation moved to the corner of Hawkstone Road and Rotherhithe Old Road, where its building was called Southwark Park Congregational Church. The old building in Derrick Street passed to the Seamen's and Boatmen's Mission, a cause very appropriate to Rotherhithe. In Lower Road, there stood two 'undenominational' missions, which were markedly successful in the late 19th and early 20th centuries. One was called St. Winifred's and was run by Henry Fuller Morriss. He began his ministry in his own house in Lower Road in 1888 and then opened a mission hall in Cathay Street two years later. He served as Mayor of Bermondsey in 1908-9 and wrote two books relating to the borough. The other mission in Lower Road, the Rotherhithe Free Church, was run by Thomas Richardson at the turn of the century. His success led him to build the Rotherhithe Great Hall in 1906 near St. Olave's Hospital. This was a substantial building and a landmark in Lower Road until it was bombed in the Second World War. A smaller building eventually replaced it. A further independent evangelist, Reuben Harris, set up a church and Sunday school in Paradise Street which he called the Ark. It was widely known earlier last century. Three Roman Catholic churches were built in Rotherhithe in Victorian and Edwardian times. The oldest was the Church of Our Lady of the Immaculate Conception, Bryan Road, dating from 1858. A girls' home and a convent under the dedication of St. Pelagius were associated with it. Bombing destroyed the church and it was not replaced until 1987-8 (in St. Elmos Road). F.W. Tasker designed the churches of St. Peter and the Guardian Angels in Paradise Street (opened in 1902) and St. Gertrude in Debnams Road (opened in 1903).

A distinctive group of churches at Rotherhithe for more than a century has been the trio of Scandinavian and Baltic churches. The presence in Rotherhithe of large numbers of mariners from Scandinavia and Finland as a result of the timber trade led to missions being set up for them near the docks in the 19th century. An old picture of the entrance to Station Yard in Lower Road, which has been reproduced frequently in recent years, is interesting chiefly because there is a notice fixed to the fence to direct mariners towards the Swedish church.

The entrance to Station Yard, Surrey Commercial Docks, 1907. A notice giving directions to the Swedish Seamen's Church is fixed to the fence on the left.

The Norwegians led the way when they set up Ebenezer Church in Redriff Road in 1871. At that time Norway was united to Sweden; the two countries separated in 1905. In 1927 a new and much grander church was built next to the entrance to Rotherhithe Tunnel. The new building justified its uncommonly fine location by proving to be a handsome landmark. It was erected by Norwegian shipowners as a memorial to 2,101 Norwegian seamen who had been killed in the First World War, and was named St. Olav's after the first Christian King of Norway in the 11th century. (St. Olave's Hospital commemorated the same individual, via the ancient Southwark church of that name.) In recent years the area in front of the church, which was enlarged through the re-alignment of

Lower Road, has been named St. Olav's Square. The church's five-bay entrance front would be judged domestic in style, were it not for the tower which rises from the centre and has a spire with a ship for a vane. The main entrance leads into a hall or meeting room, and the church proper is at the back of it. So the interior also mixes the domestic and the ecclesiastical. The church figured much in the national press in April and May, 1940, when Hitler's forces invaded Norway and it served as a rallying-point for resistance.

The Finnish Church is the second building along Albion Street from St. Olav's. This replaced a church in Stepney in 1958. The style is decidedly modern, but once again the domestic aspect is strong. From Albion Street, the building appears to be a small block of flats. A different story is told by the huge south window and by the conspicuous, detached bellcote. The apparently domestic element in these buildings arises from their range of functions. In addition to including churches, they each house the work of a travel agency, a poste restante, a left luggage office, an accommodation agency and a translation service. Their magazines keep considerable numbers of people informed of the work undertaken, many of whom live far from Rotherhithe.

The third building in this group, the Swedish Church, stands in Lower Road, next to Southwark Park. The mission took over the premises of Rotherhithe Library after the latter had moved in 1905. In 1965-6 there was a rebuilding; the new church was consecrated in October, 1966, in the presence of King Gustav Adolf of Sweden. The scale of the building is small, but it still manages to include a spire.

Two centres of social service need to be added to the long list of churches and missions. One is the Docklands Settlement. Reginald Kennedy Cox made the former Norwegian Church in Redriff Road into the fourth branch of an organisation which operated throughout the old dock areas of London. The other body is the Time and Talents Association, which began its work in Bermondsey in 1887 and has had various premises in Rotherhithe since then. In recent years it has occupied the restored mortuary in St. Marychurch Street, which was built for its original purpose in 1895.

This chapter began with charitable schools and it will end with a glance at the wider history of charities in Rotherhithe. An old parish usually has a long list of charities which were founded or augmented between the 16th and 19th centuries. The list is often to be found inscribed on large boards in the parish church, and this is the case at St. Mary's. Property given or bequeathed to a parish for charitable purposes was held either in land or in government stock (usually 'consols', meaning consolidated annuities, which yield a fixed interest and have no redemption date). Often, several gifts would be put together as they were for the same purpose (typically 'for the poor'), and so an estate might be bought with the whole. In the case of Rotherhithe, various gifts in the mid-17th century, of which those from Captain William Stephens and from Captain Roger Tweedy were the most important, were used to buy two parcels of land at Stratford and Plaistow in east London in 1659. To this day there is a Redriff Road at Plaistow in witness of this old link. Many Rotherhithe records refer to the estate, especially in the late 19th and early 20th centuries, when the buildings on it were ageing and in need of repair. There were constant discussions of possible new leases, rebuilding schemes and repairs. One scheme, for example, involved the building of six shops in the High Street at Stratford in 1899-1902. The income from the Stratford Estate and from other sources was used for two and a half centuries to buy bread to distribute to Rotherhithe's poor. In the 20th century, the income was applied to pensions instead. Another charity was known as the Coat and Cloak Charity, for it was founded in 1839 to provide 'good dark blue great coats or cloaks with hoods' for up to eight poor parishioners. As so often at Rotherhithe, there was a maritime connection: watermen and their wives or widows were to have preference. The founders of this charity were the daughters of Francis Theodore Hay (see chapter 6), the eminent wharfinger.

In 1905 many of the local bequests were put together as the Rotherhithe Consolidated Charities, which still administers the benevolence of past centuries.

11. The Redevelopment of Rotherhithe

Most parts of London have seen redevelopment since 1945 as a result of wartime bombing and of changing economic patterns, but the changes which have occurred in the districts that made up the prewar Port of London are of an altogether more drastic order than those elsewhere. The chapter on the Surrey Docks has recounted how new methods of handling cargo and a huge increase in the size of ships sent Rotherhithe's staple trades downstream, leaving a massive area of docks and wharves redundant. In addition, the growth of road transport at the expense of transport by railway and by river, tended to drive out industries which came to prefer good road access. No doubt there was also a bandwagon effect: industrial decline discourages survivors.

A summary account of Rotherhithe's recent redevelopment necessarily divides into two parts: changes up to 1981, and changes which took place after that date under the aegis of the London Docklands Development Corporation. This corporation was set up by the central government to override the planning powers of the boroughs of the former dock areas. From 1981 until December 20th, 1996, the corporation considered all the building schemes put forward for Rotherhithe. It was originally suggested that the corporation was needed because too little had been done to revive derelict areas. In the case of Rotherhithe, this view undoubtedly belittled what Southwark Council had done until 1981. The draining of most of the docks, and the laying out of roads and services, had to precede the more noticeable phase of redevelopment, in which new buildings were erected and derelict areas returned to life. One criticism which may be made of the process in most of its phases is that there was a tendency to favour large-scale schemes. Planning can stop particular patterns, but it cannot make others happen. Those which would naturally occur without encouragement would generally be small-scale. In the days before modern planning, industrial growth was almost always a jigsaw of small developments rather than a story of a few large-scale enterprises. The Surrey Docks themselves came from several disparate initiatives. At times, redevelopment has arguably been an anti-commercial process. An obvious example was the refusal in the 1980s to accommodate the haulage firms such as WBS Transport which had survived around the former docks. The comment that a barge-repairing works at 93-97 Rotherhithe Street was 'very noisy' could only have been made by somebody who had no sympathy with industrial Rotherhithe. Then there was the aspect of social change. The remark made on behalf of the development corporation in respect of Charlie Lunn's cafe on the Redriff Estate that 'there's no room any more for a working man's cafe' was decidedly dismissive of the area's traditions.

The historic centre of Rotherhithe around St. Mary's Church has seen, appropriately, the most restoration of existing buildings, chiefly wharves, in contrast to replacement building. Elsewhere, very few old buildings have been retained. In the whole of Rotherhithe Street beyond the former Surrey Lock, the only significant survivors among commercial and public buildings are Globe Wharf, Canada Wharf, the fire station at Pageant's Wharf and buildings in and around Nelson Dock. To these survivors we must add the whole of Greenland and South Docks, part of Lavender Dock plus the Lavender Pump House, the Surrey Basin (now Surrey Water), part of Canada Dock and the former dock offices near Lower Road. A great deal of the attraction of the new developments lies in their proximity to water. Without such settings, the impression given would be bleaker.

New houses and flats account for the greater part of Rotherhithe's redevelopment by area. Commercial and industrial use is much less prominent, although it is true that more such use might yet emerge in the centre of the peninsula. Upon first consideration, it is surprising that commerce and industry is found inland rather than in the detached strip along the riverfront or in the vicinity of the surviving docks. The preference of industry for road transport, however, plus the value of settings by water to sell houses and flats, explain the geography of redevelopment.

A tour of new Rotherhithe might conveniently divide into three: Rotherhithe Street; Redriff Road and Greenland Dock; and the centre of the peninsula. If we begin in Rotherhithe Street at its western end, the first landmark to notice is Corbett's Wharf. This was converted into flats by Michael Baumgarten in 1983. A traditional wharf was saved by private expenditure, which necessarily dictated the sale of the new flats at high prices to outsiders. This was criticised at the time, but without that expenditure the wharf would probably have gone. Opposite, there is a different type of conversion: the renovated blocks of the Millpond Estate. The estate was built before the war by Bermondsey Borough Council and certainly needed restoration by the 1980s. The external changes made to these blocks are paralleled elsewhere in Rotherhithe Street: a new architectural treatment to the entrances and stairways, new windows, new roofs, and measures to improve the appearance of the immediate surroundings. Similar work was carried out on the block in Cathay Street, where a particularly pleasing feature is the shield of arms of the old Borough of Bermondsey over the doors at each end. This block faces the visible foundations of King Edward III's mansion. The south side of this site has lately been used to build terraced houses: a revival of a normal urban housing type from before the First World War.

The riverfront in this vicinity is open except for the Angel and the tall, lonely building which is 1 Fulford Street. To the south there is rather rough parkland back to Jamaica Road. All this constituted a scheme which was earlier and quite separate from the redevelopment of the docks. Long ago the London County Council proposed to extend Southwark Park to the river, and this idea was more or less completed in 1979, under the Greater London Council. It was accompanied by the widening of parts of Jamaica Road and Lower Road, and the building of a large roundabout opposite the entrance to Rotherhithe Tunnel. This scheme was enormously destructive and might be considered the least acceptable of all the postwar changes in Rotherhithe. It razed most of the western part of Rotherhithe's historic centre. Mayflower Street, Clark's Orchard, Fulford Street and Seven Step Alley – which were among the most ancient streets of the area – all disappeared (or practically did so); Paradise Street east of Cathay Street lost all its buildings except St. Peter's Church; the eastern part of Jamaica Road was bereft of countless shops, pubs and houses (including the house in which Lee Boo had lived), and Christ Church, and was considerably widened. It resembles a motorway rather than an urban main street. When the previous road pattern existed, there were many shops and public buildings at the eastern end of Jamaica Road and the western part of Lower Road, making the area near Rotherhithe Tunnel lively and recognisable as a town centre. Now it is almost all given over to traffic. On the riverfront affected by the scheme, it was hugely regrettable that the historic houses adjoining the Angel were demolished in the mid-1960s (except for the one property, whose owners were successful in resisting the London County Council). They formed an attractive and popular group, in which Sir John Betjeman and Anthony Armstrong-Jones once lived.

Rotherhithe Street near the Angel, 1960. These houses were demolished by the London County Council in 1964, except for the one on the left (formerly No. 41).

Of the various wharves near St. Mary's, Hope Sufferance Wharf was much in the news in the 1970s. It was acquired by the Industrial Buildings Preservation Trust in 1974 for conversion to house forty craftsmen. Southwark Council took it over in 1977. The scheme flourished for a few years but was eventually closed. A re-conversion for housing is the likely permanent solution. This would mirror the reuse of the nearby Thames Tunnel Mills by the London and Quadrant Housing Association in 1980-3. The much-admired conversion there was carried out by Hunt Thompson Associates for £2.1 million. The 80 ft. chimney was retained. Two further conversions in the area deserve to be well-known. One was the use of 99 Rotherhithe Street for the Crunchy Frog Theatre Project for a few years from 1974. Originally, it served as a studio for artists involved in animation. Nearby, Grice's Granary and Grice's Wharf were converted for use by Sands Films and for the Rotherhithe Picture Research Library.

East of Grice's Granary, in Rotherhithe Street, there are many older buildings, including the former premises of Charles Hay & Son Ltd. at No. 135. Next door there is an open space where Cumberland Wharf stood. The stretch of road eastwards to the Surrey Lock is still largely in process of development, apart from the new housing on the south side. Beyond the lock two big new buildings catch the eye: the youth hostel on the site between Rotherhithe Street and Salter Road, and the Spice Island, a public house, near the riverfront. A little farther along there are two developments with good architectural details: Tideway Court (on the south side) and Quayside Lodge, a Barratt's scheme boasting an attractive cupola (north of the road). This is where Bull Head Dock once stood. Barratt's is one of the major builders in the area, with about half a mile of the new riverfront buildings to its credit. The Amos Estate (opposite), one of Bermondsey Council's prewar estates, was bought by the development corporation in 1985 and was then converted in a similar way to the Millpond Estate. Much farther along Rotherhithe Street there is the series of developments on the waterfront, beginning with Frederick Square, opposite the Three Compasses, all with Classical pediments, arched lower windows and Georgian doorways. The architectural quality of this work is well above average. Pageant Steps, opposite Heron Place, is another new building with a cupola. Round the bend of Rotherhithe Street we come to the Holiday Inn Hotel at Nelson Dock. This was opened in 1991 as the Scandic Crown Hotel and was renamed in 1996. The developer was the Scandinavian firm, Islef, and the architects were Kjaer and Richter. A three-masted barque built in 1952 has been installed on a slipway of the old dock, a hugely agreeable touch. Downriver, we come to the Surrey Docks Farm, which occupies part of the 18th-century Wellses' shipyard. The development corporation gave £355,000 towards the costs of this popular establishment. It moved to this site in 1986.

Surrey Docks Farm definitely brings the visitor 'Downtown', where Rotherhithe Street has traditionally met Redriff Road. The principal road which reaches this junction today is Salter Road, the new ring road round most of the peninsula. It commemorates Dr. Alfred Salter, the prewar Member of Parliament for Bermondsey. Near this junction there are the renovated Redriff Estate, the Docklands Settlement, a few old public houses (with unaltered names) and some modern riverside developments. Custom House Reach was built in the 1960s, before the docks closed; the huge complex next door, New Caledonian Wharf, is much more recent.

Redriff Road is the main road from which the visitor gains access to the developments surrounding the Greenland Dock. The scale of some of these developments is considerable. The vicinity of Norway Gate is almost a new town in itself. Just upstream of Greenland Lock, there is the substantial development called Greenland Passage, in Portland stone and yellow stock brick, which was designed for Islef U.K. Ltd. by Kjaer and Richter, as in the case of Nelson Dock. Islef is a Danish company, and hence the laying of the foundation stone here by the Danish Ambassador in 1986. Greenland Dock itself is mostly surrounded by housing, and the view is enhanced by the many boats which are moored at the river end of it. Boats are particularly numerous in the adjoining South Dock, for it boasts a 250-berth marina and a watersports' centre, which opened in 1990 and for which the development corporation provided £1 million. Baltic Quay, at the west end of the dock, is a large glass-clad, steel-framed building, reflecting recent architects' fondness for the arch as a major motif.

The centre of the peninsula was perhaps most at issue in the planning debates of the 1970s and 1980s, and yet it is still the least finished part. This is not for want of money and effort, for the flagship of the developments, the Surrey Quays Shopping Centre (opened in 1988), cost £35 million. In 1998 an Underground station on the new Jubilee Line, called Canada Water, was opened nearby. This new economic centre of Rotherhithe may be reached via Surrey Quays Road, where the old economic centre – the Surrey Docks' offices of 1887 – still stand. For some years they served as the development corporation's local headquarters.

The largest commercial building beyond the shopping centre is the one belonging to Associated Newspapers, publishers of the *Daily Mail* and the *Evening Standard*. It is a printing plant, near Canada Street, which opened in 1989. In this vicinity, the Canadian connections of the old docks are kept alive. General Wolfe's capture of Quebec in 1759 underlies the new street names to an extent which would have warmed the patriotic heart of a David Garrick.

Mention was made in chapter 10 of many schools, the histories of which were recounted until early last century at the latest. Their more recent histories are parts of the story of the peninsula's redevelopment. Rotherhithe's oldest school foundation, that of Peter Hills, is now housed in a new building north of Salter Road, roughly on the site of St. Paul's Church. The new school represents also the old St. Mary's School which used to stand in Lower Road and is therefore the Church of England's primary school for Rotherhithe. Another old primary school in new premises (opened in 1990) is Redriff School, off Salter Road. This was one of the London County Council's primary schools and formerly stood in Rotherhithe Street, near the present Surrey Docks Farm. A third primary school, called Alfred Salter School, is an entirely new foundation and is yet another memorial of the good doctor. It was formally opened on October 31st, 1995, in premises whose architectural details are impressive. Nearby there is a fourth primary school, St. John's, which serves the Roman Catholic community and is run in association with the Church of Our Lady of the Immaculate Conception in St. Elmos Road. All these schools have received large grants from the development corporation, but by far the largest grant (£3.7 million) went to the area's only secondary school, Bacon's College. This is a City Technology College and represents a foundation which goes back to the early 18th century in neighbouring Bermondsey. Its present building in Timber Pond Road was opened in 1991.

Recreation has not been forgotten in the redevelopment of Rotherhithe. A large area running north-south was set aside in 1980 as the Russia Dock Woodland. Two years later the Lavender Pond Nature Park was inaugurated. This is associated with the adjoining pump house, which once kept up the water levels in the docks and is now the Rotherhithe Heritage Museum. A collection of items found by Ron Goode on the foreshore of the Thames is a key attraction. A further open space is the Stave Hill Ecological Park, extending to five and a half acres. It opened in 1986. Off Salter Road there is the Surrey Docks Stadium, which is the ground of Fisher Athletic Football Club. This ground and the watersports' centre mentioned earlier are the only major sporting facilities in the peninsula.

It remains to point out that Rotherhithe's oldest sporting venue, Southwark Park, saw a considerable development in 1980, when a new sports' complex was completed. It included an astroturf football pitch.

All these substantial developments which have been described in this chapter have altered Rotherhithe to a very great extent. Its economy, its buildings, its population and even the layout of many of its streets have changed markedly. A visitor who had last arrived in, say, the 1950s would discern only a few familiar landmarks among the new developments. These changes have been among the most momentous in Rotherhithe's history and are ones whose effects will not be fully clear for some years yet. History is truly being made in our own day.

Bibliography

The first book in any bibliography of Rotherhithe must be Edward
Josselyn Beck's *Memorials to serve for a History of the Parish of St.
Mary, Rotherhithe* (Cambridge University Press, 1907). It was the product
of a forty-year acquaintance from a privileged vantage-point. The book has
much excellent detail, especially on the Parish Church of St. Mary, its
daughter-churches, schools and local personalities of the 18th and 19th
centuries. It omits a description of much local industry, however, and it
was written without access to many sources which are available today.
Finally, the fact that it was published 90 years ago means that it does not
address such subjects as the Second World War and the great changes
which have arisen from the closure of the Surrey Commercial Docks.
The work is substantial, but not comprehensive.

Beck's predecessor as Rector of Rotherhithe, Edward Blick, wrote
*A Short Account of the Churches, Schools and Charities in the Parish
of St. Mary, Rotherhithe* (1847). It gives details of his own work from
1835 and offers historical details of some charities. A later and wide-
ranging account of local charities is provided in *Endowed Charities
(County of London)*, Vol. II, compiled by the Charity Commission and
published by order of Parliament in 1899.

Further general accounts of Rotherhithe's history are given in the
Victoria County History of Surrey, Vol. IV (Constable & Co. Ltd.,
1912; the section on Rotherhithe is by Helen Douglas-Irvine, pp. 83-92);
Colonel M.B. Pearson, *The Parish of Rotherhithe* (1912); and *Old
Rotherhithe* by Leonard Hobbs (unpublished typescript in Southwark
Local Studies Library, dated 1931). The latter is not a fluent narrative
history, but it has many interesting oddments. The 20th-century story of
the area, up to 1965, is given in V. Leff and C.H. Blunden, *Riverside
Story/The Story of Bermondsey and its People* (Civic Publicity Services
Ltd., c. 1965). It is chiefly an account of municipal government, that is,
of Bermondsey Borough Council. Rotherhithe's wartime experience is
described in James D. Stewart, *Bermondsey in War 1939-1945*
(Bermondsey and Rotherhithe Society, 1980). The career of Dr. Alfred
Salter is recounted in Fenner Brockway, *Bermondsey Story/The Life of
Alfred Salter* (reprinted by Stephen Humphrey, 1995). Life in the

Downtown district earlier this century is agreeably described by F. Mary Wilson in *Between Bridgers* (Copyrights Ltd., 1966).

Useful general information can be obtained from the *Bermondsey Official Guides* (various editions until 1963) and from the *Southwark Annual* (1893-1906). Old pictures may be seen in Stephen Humphrey, *Southwark, Bermondsey and Rotherhithe in Old photographs* (Sutton Publishing Ltd., 1995), and in Peter Marcan, *A Bermondsey and Rotherhithe Album* (Peter Marcan publications, 1992). Old 25-inch Ordnance Survey maps of the district have been reproduced by Alan Godfrey as *Rotherhithe 1894* (Alan Godfrey, 1986) and *Rotherhithe 1914* (Alan Godfrey, 1984). Adjoining sheets are under the titles of *Bermondsey and Wapping* and *Deptford (North)*. The Port of London Authority's map of the Surrey Commercial Docks in 1955 has been reproduced by Edward Stanford (1987).

A good introduction to the history of the docks is found in John Pudney, *London's Docks* (Thames and Hudson Ltd., 1975). Illustrations of that history are provided in Chris Ellmers and Alex Werner, *Dockland Life/A Pictorial History of London's Docks 1860-1970* (Mainstream Publishing Co. (Edinburgh) Ltd., 1991). The early history of Rotherhithe's docks is covered by Nathaniel Gould, *Historical Notice of the Commercial Docks* (1844) and by Josiah Griffin, *History of the Surrey Commercial Docks* (1877). The wider history of the Port of London is recounted in James Bird, *The Geography of the Port of London* (Hutchinson University Library, 1957), which was published when the upriver port was still flourishing. The prewar atmosphere of the port is splendidly described in A.G. Linney, *The Peepshow of the Port of London* (Sampson Low, Marston & Co. Ltd., c. 1929). The author was the editor of the *P.L.A. Monthly*, a journal which first appeared in 1925 and is itself an excellent source for life in the docks. A snapshot of the riverfront in 1937 is provided in Chris Ellmers and Alex Werner, *London's Lost Riverscape* (Penguin Group, 1988); this consists of photographs of the riverfront on both banks from London Bridge downstream to Greenwich, taken for the Port of London Authority in 1937, and gives attention to the wharves (which are otherwise neglected). The docker's lot is well described in Tom Ash, *Childhood Days/The Docks and Dock Slang* (published by the author, 1982; 4th edition, 1994). Life on the river a century ago is the subject of Harry Harris,

Under Oars/Reminiscences of a Thames Lighterman 1894-1909
(Centreprise Trust Ltd., 1988). Also of great value is *Dockland/An
Illustrated Historical Survey of Life and Work in East London* (North
East London Polytechnic, 1986).

The essential book about shipbuilding on the Thames is Philip Banbury,
Shipbuilders of the Thames and Medway (David and Charles
(Publishers) Ltd., 1971). The local story is recounted in Stuart Rankin,
Shipbuilding in Rotherhithe/An Historical Introduction (Dockside
Studio, 1996) and the same author's *Shipbuilding in Rotherhithe – The
Nelson Dockyard* (Dockside Studio, 1996). He has written several more
short accounts of the subject. An exhaustive account of the *Temeraire*
and a good discussion of shipbreaking generally at Rotherhithe are found
in Judy Egerton, *Making and Meaning/Turner/The Fighting Temeraire*
(National Gallery Publications Ltd., 1995).

Mary Boast's booklet, *The Mayflower and Pilgrim Story/Chapters from
Rotherhithe and Southwark* (Southwark Council, 1970; revised edition,
1995) gives a full and judicious account of Rotherhithe's connections
with that great expedition. The story of Lee Boo is the subject of Daniel
J. Peacock's relatively recent book, *Lee Boo of Belau/A Prince in
London* (South Sea Books, Honolulu, 1987). The Southwark Local
Studies Library also holds books which were written in the late 18th and
early 19th centuries about Captain Wilson's voyages by his
contemporaries, such as George Keate's *An Account of the Pelew
Islands* (2nd edition, 1788). The Thames Tunnel is discussed in Paul
Clements, *Marc Isambard Brunel* (Longmans, Green & Co. Ltd., 1970);
John Pudney, *Brunel and His World* (Thames and Hudson Ltd., 1974);
L.T.C. Rolt, *Isambard Kingdom Brunel* (Longmans, Green & Co. Ltd.,
1974); and David Lampe, *The Tunnel* (George G. Harrap & Co. Ltd.,
1963). The Rotherhithe Tunnel is described in E.H. Tabor, *The
Rotherhithe Tunnel* (taken from Engineering Wonders of the World,
1910) and in *Opening of the Rotherhithe Tunnel* (London County
Council, 1908). Rotherhithe's gas works are described and illustrated in
Rotherhithe Works (South Metropolitan Gas Co., 1948). The building of
King Edward III's mansion is recounted in Howard Colvin, *History of
the King's Works*, Vol. 2 (1963), pp. 989-994.

Francis Culling Carr-Gomm's edition of the *Letters and Journals of Field Marshal Sir William Maynard Gomm, G.C.B. ... from 1799 to Waterloo, 1815* (John Murray, 1881) is a valuable source for Rotherhithe's best-known landlord. The Field-Marshal's great-great-nephew, Richard Carr-Gomm, wrote *Push on the Door/An Autobiography* (Carr-Gomm Society Ltd., 1979), which gives the story of his founding two housing associations in the area.

The original parish registers of St. Mary's are now kept in the London Metropolitan Archives at Clerkenwell (40 Northampton Road, London, EC1R OHB). The same repository holds the records of the Bermondsey Board of Guardians, which administered the Victorian and later Poor Law in Rotherhithe. The Southwark Local Studies Library (211 Borough High Street, London, SE1 1JA) holds the vestry minutes, rate books and Victorian administrative records of the civil parish of St. Mary, Rotherhithe, plus minute books of the two oldest schools, deeds of the Carr-Gomm Estate and numerous further deeds and sale catalogues of properties throughout the district. These primary sources are particularly valuable when they are studied in conjunction with the more general literature detailed above.

Index